HYPOCRISY

HYPOCRISY

MORAL FRAUD AND OTHER VICES

JAMES S. SPIEGEL

Baker Books

A Division of Baker Book House Co
Grand Rapids, Michigan 49516

Published by Baker Books
a division of Baker Book House Company
P.O. Box 6287, Grand Rapids, MI 49516–6287

Printed in the United States of America

Library of Congress Cataloging-in-Publication Data

Spiegel, James S., 1963–
    Hypocrisy : moral fraud and other vices / James S. Spiegel.
        p.   cm.
    Includes bibliographical references and index.
    ISBN 0-8010-6046-X (pbk.)
    1. Hypocrisy. I. Title.
BJ1535.H8S65   1999
179'.8—dc21   99-35083

For current information about all releases from Baker Book House, visit our web site:

http://www.bakerbooks.com

Contents

Acknowledgments   7
Introduction   9

1. The Mother of All Vices: Historical
   Background   13
2. A Lie Told by Outward Deeds: Defining
   Hypocrisy   25
3. Taking Oneself In: Self-Deception   44
4. The Spirit Is Willing: Moral Weakness   68
5. The Now and the Not Yet: Sin, Self-Control,
   and Sanctification   87
6. Cheating at the Goodness Stakes: A Moral
   Analysis of Hypocrisy   105
7. At Least I'm Not a Hypocrite: The Apologetic Problem
   of Hypocrisy   126
   Conclusion   145

Notes   149
Bibliography   164
Index   169

Acknowledgments

I have many people to thank for their help on this book. In addition to formal comments on the manuscript during its evolution, I have received personal encouragement from many good friends who saw the merit of this project early on. Doug Geivett, Paul House, Eric Johnson, Jason Loftis, Robert Moore-Jumonville, Dan Newcomb, Steve Norman, and Ryan Spence have helped me in ways of which they might not be fully aware. I have benefited as well from critical comments made by scholars who attended my paper presentations on hypocrisy at meetings of the Society of Christian Philosophers and the Evangelical Philosophical Society. And for their extensive editorial suggestions I thank Erin Carter and Stephen Webb.

I thank my colleagues in the Biblical Studies, Christian Education and Philosophy department at Taylor University for providing me with reliable professional guidance. And my gratitude extends to many others in the Taylor community. Joanne Cosgrove in particular has personified efficiency and grace in tracking down hundreds of books and articles for me. And Kari Manganello and Carolyn Webb were a great help in compiling the bibliography. I am also deeply appreciative of the staff at Baker, especially Jim Weaver, with whom it has been a joy to work.

I also thank my family, without whose support I would have accomplished nothing. First and foremost, I thank my wife Amy who has taken joy in tasks connected with this book that others would have viewed as burdensome. She has contributed in many ways to this project and fertilized my thinking on a variety of subjects. Thanks to her, my ideas for scholarly projects continue to multiply. I am also thankful to my brother Robert whose professional counsel, personal encouragement, and inspiration as a fellow writer have proved invaluable. And I thank my parents, who are living models of integrity and moral strength, the very antithesis of the vices discussed in this book. From my father I learned what it means to live in a morally principled way. From my mother I learned the value of wonder and inquiry. It is to them that this book is dedicated.

Introduction

When I was a young teenager I would often mow lawns for extra cash. On one occasion a friend and I approached a man who lived across the street from my house and asked him if he would allow us to cut his lawn. He agreed and offered to pay us twenty-five dollars for the job, noting that he would be gone for the weekend and would therefore pay us upon his return. That Saturday my friend and I worked for several hours, but because it was a rather large lawn, we had to finish it on Sunday. The next day we returned to obtain our wages from the man. In hopes that he would be impressed by our labor, we informed him that it took us two days to get the job done. "Two days?" he asked. "You mean to tell me that you mowed my lawn on Sunday?" We nodded. "Well, boys, I don't allow work to be done at my house on Sundays. I can't pay you." We watched him as he dug into his pocket and pulled out approximately two dollars in change. He handed it to us, saying, "I'm doing this out of the kindness of my heart."

In stunned silence my friend and I sauntered back into my house and informed my father as to what had just transpired. He was irate. "Hypocrites . . . lousy hypocrites!" he bellowed. "They smile so sweetly and look so righteous at church, but in the real world they're nothing but swindlers and cheats!" It is my earliest and most vivid memory of hypocrisy. And it was the first time I saw my dad overtly express his frustration over hypocrites in the church. Since that experience, he has repeatedly voiced his complaint about religious people who fail to practice what they preach. And he is quick to remind others that although he falls short of certain moral ideals, "at least I am not a hypocrite."

While this anecdote is disturbing, it will hardly be a revelation to the reader that Christians sometimes fail to practice what they preach. The forms of hypocrisy we encounter in the church are as varied as sin itself, and there is no vice so severe that no Christian has fallen into it. And yet, it is one of the central teachings of the New Testament that to know Christ is to be changed for the better morally. How can these facts coincide? This is what may be called the "problem of hypocrisy" for the Christian apologist. I have heard that next to the problem of evil, this is the most commonly cited reason for rejecting the Christian faith. While apologists have done a tremendous amount of helpful work in dealing with the problem of evil, very little has been written on the problem of hypocrisy. I find this appalling. A major philosophical and psychological stumbling block lies in the path of countless seekers, and we have virtually ignored it. Judging by the literature, it seems that Christian apologists think it more worthwhile to dispute the technical minutiae of natural theology than even to address the charge that hypocritical Christians render the gospel message null and void.

To diminish sin in the church would go a long way in alleviating the problem of hypocrisy in the church. But alas, as long as there is sin, there will be hypocrites. So how are Christians to respond to the skeptic's complaint in the meantime? This book is, in part, intended to provide just such a response. But there is much else I have to say in this book that I hope to be both interesting and valuable. So the six chapters preceding my treatment of the apologetic problem of hypocrisy ought not to be seen as merely preparatory for that task. To define hypocrisy (as I attempt to do in chap. 2) is as important an endeavor as it is difficult. Issues in the philosophy and psychology of self-deception (chap. 3) are fascinating and profitable for appreciating the complexity and mystery of the human mind. Readers may benefit in a practical way from the two chapters dealing with moral weakness (chaps. 4 and 5). And the moral analysis of hypocrisy is essential for raising our awareness as to precisely why hypocrisy is wrong (chap. 6).

This is a text that aims to accomplish much, as it constitutes a three-fold analysis of hypocrisy. It analyzes the concept philosophically, psychologically, and theologically. And I do not pretend to have expert credentials in all of these areas of scholarship. My formal training is principally in philosophy. Still I hope that my treatment is a competent one, however superficial it might prove to be in some areas. This book should not be conceived as the definitive statement or final word on hypocrisy from the standpoint of Christian scholarship. It is better conceived as a prolegomenon, an introduction to the wide range of issues pertaining to the phenomenon of hypocrisy and, if nothing else, a call to fellow Christian scholars to take up the task of addressing them in a rigorous way. Brothers and sisters, when it comes to this topic, we have been sleeping far too long.

The Mother of All Vices

Historical Background

Man is no angel. He is sometimes more of a hypocrite and sometimes less, and then fools say that he has or has not principles.

Amos Bronson Alcott

O, what may man within him hide, / Though angel on the outward side.

Shakespeare

Almost daily, reports of hypocrisy make their way into the news. A respected legislator is found guilty of shady financial dealings. An admired sports or entertainment personality is busted for drug possession. Or a pastor confesses to lewd sexual conduct. We are all familiar with the dozens of high profile figures whose names have become synonymous with hypocrisy in recent years. But the phenomenon is nothing new. Every era has its exemplars.

Derived from the Greek *hypokrisia,* meaning "to play a part on stage," hypocrisy is defined generally as the failure to practice what one preaches. But the concept is much more complex than this popular definition would suggest. Before trying to define hypocrisy, however, let's look at a few cases of hypocrisy in classic literature and the Bible.

LITERARY EXAMPLES OF HYPOCRISY

Moliere's Tartuffe is a religious hypocrite of the highest order. He convinces the wealthy Orgon that he is a holy man through outward displays of religious devotion. Tartuffe prays ostentatiously, proclaims his disdain for worldly goods, and serves others with exaggerated humility. Orgon is taken in by the facade, and he testifies to Tartuffe's devotion as follows:

> He used to come into our church each day
> And humbly kneel nearby, and start to pray.
> He'd draw the eyes of everybody there
> By the deep fervor of his heartfelt prayer;
> He'd sigh and weep, and sometimes with a sound
> Of rapture he would bend and kiss the ground;
> And when I rose to go, he'd run before
> To offer me holy-water at the door.
> His serving-man, no less devout than he,
> Informed me of his master's poverty;
> I gave him gifts, but in his humbleness
> He'd beg me every time to give him less.
> "Oh, that's too much," he'd cry, "too much by twice!
> I don't deserve it. The half, Sir, would suffice."
> And when I wouldn't take it back, he'd share
> Half of it with the poor, right then and there.
> At length, Heaven prompted me to take him in
> To dwell with us, and free our souls from sin.[1]

Tartuffe's ruse earns him a place in Orgon's household, where he also convinces Orgon's mother, Madame Pernelle, and wife, Elmire, of his piety. But gradually Tartuffe's hypocrisy is exposed as his lust gets the better of him, and he audaciously propositions Elmire. Orgon's son, Damis, witnesses this attempt to seduce his mother and boldly accuses Tartuffe to his father. Orgon is incredulous, being thoroughly duped by Tartuffe's religiosity. He turns on his son, disinheriting him because of his apparent slander. On top of this, he makes Tartuffe the sole heir of his estate.

Only after the legal papers have been signed does Orgon become aware of Tartuffe's hypocrisy, as he secretly witnesses his sexual advances on Elmire, made with an elaborate justification of his lewd behavior:

> Some joys, its true, are wrong in Heaven's eyes;
> Yet Heaven is not averse to compromise;
> There is a science, lately formulated,
> Whereby one's conscience may be liberated,
> And any wrongful act you care to mention
> May be redeemed by purity of intention.
> I'll teach you, Madam, the secrets of that science;
> Meanwhile, just place on me your full reliance.[2]

Orgon confronts Tartuffe and demands that he leave the premises. Tartuffe scoffs, reminding Orgon that now he, Tartuffe, is legal owner of the property and that it is Orgon and his kin who must leave. In the end only through a royal edict is Tartuffe's injustice defeated. The king restores Orgon's estate to him and has Tartuffe imprisoned.

Several features of this story are worth highlighting. Note, first, that Tartuffe seems to be quite aware of his own pretense. His actions are deliberate, aiming all along at personal gain, his sham piety but a means to that end. Second, Tartuffe's ploy is not sporadic but sustained. For his plan to succeed, he must always appear humble and generous before Orgon, at least until he secures the object of his lust. And last, when Tartuffe's hypocrisy is finally exposed, he is unrepentant. Rather than admitting his shameful behavior and seeking forgiveness, he is indignant and utterly resistant to moral change.

Judge Jaffrey Pyncheon in Hawthorne's *House of the Seven Gables* is another classic hypocrite. A man of social and political eminence, he is superficially virtuous—publicly respected for his patriotism, civic-mindedness, and church service. Personally, Pyncheon charms with a gleaming smile, cheerful manner, and a general air of benevolence. But this is all for show. His outward virtue is a thin veneer masking a sinister heart. His affability can as quickly turn "acrid and disagree-

able." Ambition and an insatiable thirst for wealth characterize the real Judge Pyncheon, and his greed prompts him to
do vicious things. To secure land for himself, he has his own
cousin Clifford convicted for a murder he did not commit.
After thirty years Pyncheon has him released in an act of apparent mercy. In reality, the judge aims to use the opportunity to extort information from Clifford regarding his deceased
uncle's treasure, on threat of having him committed to an
insane asylum. However, Judge Pyncheon dies suddenly and
mysteriously before his blackmail can work. Clifford gloats
over the corpse of his cruel cousin, finding a macabre satisfaction in the old hypocrite's demise.

Pyncheon's hypocrisy is more subtle and complex than that
of Tartuffe. Like Tartuffe's, Pyncheon's pretense is sustained
and self-serving, yet it is different in that it is not clear to what
extent, if at all, Pyncheon is aware of his own pretense. Although his evil deeds are intentional, it is possible that he does
not intend his politeness and social grace as a sham, unlike
Tartuffe, who is fully aware that his actions are pretentious. The
difference in the self-awareness of these two hypocrites (if there
is a difference) might owe to the fact that Tartuffe plays the part
of a supremely holy man, while Pyncheon's is a pretense of
mere social and moral decency. The more extreme one's ploy,
the more deliberate its execution is likely to be.

One of the most famous hypocrites in nineteenth century literature is the slimy Uriah Heep in Dickens' *David Copperfield.*
The novel traces the development of the book's namesake,
who after a tumultuous youth eventually boards with a family
called the Wickfields. Mr. Wickfield has a legal practice, and
David is hired to work in the law office. Uriah Heep is a clerk
for Mr. Wickfield who denies his secret ambitions for power,
declaring himself "too humble." In spite of his protests of humility and general facade of innocence, hints of Heep's true character appear in his "shadowless eyes and cadaverous face." He
soon proves to be a corrupt opportunist, exploiting Wickfield's
drinking excesses to his own advantage and eventually insin-
uating himself into a partnership in the law practice.

As in *Tartuffe* and *House of the Seven Gables,* the hypocrite
of *David Copperfield* gets his due. Near the end of the tale,
Heep is confronted with irrefutable evidence that he is "a

fraudulent cheat," guilty of forgery and embezzlement. But Heep refuses to confess. Instead, he stiffens and responds with threats. Ultimately, his treachery brings him only disgrace, as he is imprisoned for his crimes, a just reward for "the most consummate villain that ever existed."

Uriah Heep, it appears, is more like Tartuffe with regard to the degree of self-awareness implicit in his hypocrisy. And like both Tartuffe and Pyncheon, Heep's fraud is sustained over a long period of time, and he is unrepentant when reproved for his evil ways.

BIBLICAL EXAMPLES OF HYPOCRISY

Biblical narrative offers some striking candidates for hypocrisy. Consider Saul, who issued a royal decree banning the consultation of spiritists and expelling them from the land. In the face of the impending threat of Israel's enemies, Saul became fearful and desperate enough to contradict his own law:

> When Saul saw the Philistine army, he was afraid; terror filled his heart. He inquired of the LORD, but the LORD did not answer him by dreams or Urim or prophets. Saul then said to his attendants, "Find me a woman who is a medium, so I may go and inquire of her."
>
> "There is one in Endor," they said.
>
> So Saul disguised himself, putting on other clothes, and at night he and two men went to the woman. "Consult a spirit for me," he said, "and bring up for me the one I name."
>
> But the woman said to him, "Surely you know what Saul has done. He has cut off the mediums and spiritists from the land. Why have you set a trap for my life to bring about my death?"
>
> Saul swore to her by the LORD, "As surely as the LORD lives, you will not be punished for this."[3]

This incident is complicated by the fact that Saul's inconsistent behavior is precipitated by fear, as "terror filled his heart" with the approach of the Philistine army. Such a situation might be seen at least as a mitigating circumstance for acting inconsistently with one's own convictions. In fact, Saul might better be described as morally weak than as a hypocrite.

Saul's successor, David, is a more likely candidate for hypocrisy. After seducing Bathsheba and plotting the death of her husband, Uriah the Hittite,

> The LORD sent Nathan to David. When he came to him, he said, "There were two men in a certain town, one rich and the other poor. The rich man had a very large number of sheep and cattle, but the poor man had nothing except one little ewe lamb he had bought. He raised it, and it grew up with him and his children. It shared his food, drank from his cup and even slept in his arms. It was like a daughter to him.
>
> "Now a traveler came to the rich man, but the rich man refrained from taking one of his own sheep or cattle to prepare a meal for the traveler who had come to him. Instead, he took the ewe lamb that belonged to the poor man and prepared it for the one who had come to him."
>
> David burned with anger against the man and said to Nathan, "As surely as the LORD lives, the man who did this deserves to die! He must pay for that lamb four times over, because he did such a thing and had no pity."[4]
>
> Then Nathan said to David, "You are the man!"[5]

David fits the profile of the classic hypocrite better than Saul, for his action does not seem to be motivated by fear or any other overwhelming passion. Yet, unlike Tartuffe, Pyncheon, and Uriah Heep, David is not aware of his duplicity, that is until he is confronted by Nathan. Moreover, and most significant, when David's sin is plainly exposed to him, he does repent.

Finally, in the New Testament we find Peter professing to Jesus,

> "Even if all fall away on account of you, I never will."
>
> "I tell you the truth," Jesus answered, "this very night before the rooster crows, you will disown me three times."
>
> But Peter declared, "Even if I have to die with you, I will never disown you."

Jesus is arrested and brought before the Sanhedrin to be tried. And as he had predicted, all the disciples flee.

Now Peter was sitting out in the courtyard, and a servant girl came to him, "You also were with Jesus of Galilee," she said.

But he denied it before them all. "I don't know what you're talking about," he said.

Then he went out to the gateway, where another girl saw him and said to the people there, "This fellow was with Jesus of Nazareth."

He denied it again, with an oath: "I don't know the man!"

After a little while, those standing there went up to Peter and said, "Surely you are one of them, for your accent gives you away."

Then he began to call down curses on himself and he swore to them, "I don't know the man!"

Immediately a rooster crowed. Then Peter remembered the word Jesus had spoken: "Before the rooster crows, you will disown me three times." And he went outside and wept bitterly.[6]

Peter's denial represents yet another complex case that does not fall easily into the category of hypocrisy. Although the disciple fails to practice what he preaches (and sincerely believes), his inconsistency is neither persistent, resistant to correction, nor deliberate. Like Saul, Peter seems overcome by fear, specifically that his association with Jesus would endanger him. Also like Saul's, Peter's actions are not part of a long-term pattern of deceit. His inconsistency is brief, a serious but momentary lapse into cowardice. And like David, Peter repents as soon as he recognizes his offense. In all these respects, Peter differs fundamentally from the likes of Tartuffe, Pyncheon, and Uriah Heep.

A Survey of Philosophical and Theological Reflections on Hypocrisy

In each of the above cases, someone fails to practice what he preaches, yet these narratives differ vastly in how this discrepancy is manifested. They begin to show just how complex the concept of hypocrisy is and suggest that arriving at a satisfactory definition of this vice will not be easy.

Thinkers from the ancient world to contemporary times have tried their hand at defining the term. One of the earliest descriptions of hypocrisy is found in Plato's *Republic,* where Glaucon provides a profile of the unjust man:

> In the first place, the unjust man must act as clever crafts-men do. A first-rate pilot or physician, for example, feels the difference between impossibilities and possibilities in his art and attempts the one and lets the others go, and then, too, if he does happen to trip, he is equal to correcting his error. Sim-ilarly, the unjust man who attempts injustice rightly must be supposed to escape detection if he is to be altogether unjust, and we must regard the man who is caught as a bungler. For the height of injustice is to seem just without being so. To the perfectly unjust man, then, we must assign perfect injustice and withhold nothing of it, but we must allow him, while com-mitting the greatest wrongs, to have secured for himself the greatest reputation for justice. . . .[7]

Although the term is not used in this passage, the vice Glaucon describes is clearly hypocrisy. The unjust person makes a practice of appearing to be much better than he really is. Justice is generally defined as "giving to each its due." On Glaucon's account, then, hypocrisy is a species of injustice precisely because the hypocrite does not get his due for the wrongs he commits. Such injustice is evident in the actions of Tartuffe, Pyncheon, and Uriah Heep. And it is their prolonged success in profiting from their injustice that makes their hypocrisy so despicable (and, from a literary standpoint, compelling).

Aquinas regarded hypocrisy or "dissimulation" as "a lie told by the signs of outward deeds," such as when one pretends to have a good intention in performing an action, when in fact the intention is corrupt.[8] Ordinarily, a deed is a sign of the person's intentions. Not so for the hypocrite, who "by out-ward signs of deeds or things . . . signifies that which he is not."[9] Unlike other vices, dissimulation is not opposed to a particular virtue, not even the one the hypocrite pretends to perform. Rather, it is opposed to truth itself. Hypocrisy, Aquinas says, is a complex vice, for it is unholiness combined with a simulation of holiness.

On Aquinas's analysis, Tartuffe's lie told by his outward deeds is that he is humble with righteous intentions. Pyncheon's etiquette and personal charm falsely testify to his real nature and sinister intentions. And Uriah Heep's humble veneer obviously "signifies that which he is not." So Aquinas's definition applies readily to these classic cases, all instances of unholiness combined with an imitation of holiness. His definition would also seem to imply David was a hypocrite, since his severe judgment of the man in the prophet's parable implicitly declared David's own righteousness and so constituted a lie of sorts.

Definitions of hypocrisy such as those offered by Plato and Aquinas are helpful, as far as they go, but they do not unpack the more specific elements of hypocrisy. The German philosopher G. W. F. Hegel names three basic elements in hypocrisy. First, there is a knowledge of the moral law or what he calls "the true universal," whether this knowledge takes the form of a mere feeling of duty or a deeper understanding of what the moral law entails. Second, there is a volition or choice that conflicts with this universal. And third, the hypocrite recognizes this conflict. That is, "the conscious subject is aware in willing that his particular volition is evil."[10]

The evil content in the hypocrite's choice pertains to its falsity, and this in two senses. First, the hypocrite "hold[s] up evil as good in the eyes of others," tricking observers into thinking him good.[11] And further, by the goodness of some of his actions, words, or reasons for acting, he can justify his own evil to himself. The hypocrite is self-deceived. So the mind of the hypocrite "demonstrates its respect for duty and virtue just by making a show of them, and using them as a mask to hide itself from its own consciousness, no less than from others."[12]

The requirement that the hypocrite be aware of his deceit is a stringent one, making the qualifications for hypocrisy more narrow than those offered by Aquinas, among others. For instance, with Hegel's characterization, David would probably not qualify as a hypocrite, since he was not fully aware of his inconsistency, as is suggested by his immediate repentance when confronted. The matter of self-awareness and its relationship to morality generally and hypocritical behavior

21

in particular is complex and controversial, as our study will reveal.

Some thinkers have focused on "self-deceit" or what is sometimes called "internal hypocrisy." The eighteenth-century bishop Joseph Butler, for example, identifies the internal hypocrite as one who fails to recognize that the rules of conduct apply to himself. Such persons "think, and reason, and judge quite differently upon any matter relating to themselves from what they do in cases of others where they are not interested."[13] The two principle causes of this condition, Butler maintains, are self-absorption and self-ignorance. Self-absorbed persons have "so fixed and steady an eye upon their own interest . . . as in a manner to regard nothing else,"[14] while in others there is "a general ignorance of themselves, and wrong way of thinking and judging in everything relating to themselves; their fortune, reputation, everything in which self can come in."[15]

Butler's analysis certainly pegs the characters of the classic literary hypocrites we have discussed. It has the additional merit of explaining why such figures are resistant to correction. For, if his claim about the causes of self-deceit is correct, it is precisely those who are self-absorbed or self-ignorant who would be least able to recognize this vice in themselves. The self-deceived person, by the very nature of his vice, will be handicapped in the matter of moral self-analysis. Thus, Butler asserts that self-deceit is "a corruption of the whole moral character in its principle," because proper judgment of oneself is so essential to morality.[16]

More recently, the French philosopher Jean Paul Sartre expounded upon a form of self-deceit which he terms "bad faith." Bad faith is a sort of lie, but it is distinguished from Aquinas's application of the term by the fact that it is a lie told to oneself. Here "the one to whom the lie is told and the one who lies are one and the same person."[17] The deceiver is also the deceived, for it is from oneself that one hides some displeasing truth. But mustn't a person be aware of the truth to be able to hide the truth from oneself, thus implying that bad faith is really impossible? Such considerations led Sartre to pose a psychoanalytical interpretation of the phenomenon. The unconscious preserves "the duality between deceiver and the deceived."[18] The fears and primal desires that operate in the unconscious psyche enable the subject to at once be fully aware of her conduct and also to deceive herself about the fuller meaning of her conduct.

The account of philosopher Gilbert Ryle falls into the "internal hypocrisy" tradition as well. He suggests that to be hypocritical is to "try to appear actuated by a motive other than one's real motive."[19] (He distinguishes the hypocrite from the charlatan, on the grounds that the latter shams abilities, while the former shams intentions.) Hypocrisy is always deliberate, according to Ryle. The hypocrite self-consciously deceives others with pretenses of motives using language "calculated to give false impressions."[20]

Determining whether Tartuffe, Pyncheon, Uriah Heep, or anyone else is guilty of Sartrean bad faith or Rylean internal hypocrisy is especially difficult, because this calls for close analysis of the hidden dynamics of the mental life. As our discussion will show, the psychological, philosophical, and theological questions raised by these accounts are multiple and complex.

Conclusion and Overview

Hypocrisy is not easy to analyze. While there is consensus among key thinkers that hypocrisy is characterized by some sort of conflict or discrepancy involving human behavior, a number of issues wait to be addressed. How is hypocrisy precisely to be defined? Is there a single definition of the concept that will satisfactorily account for all its instances? These questions will occupy us in the next chapter.

There are also psychological questions to address. Does hypocrisy always or ever involve self-deception? If so, how are we to conceive of self-deception? Is such a thing even possible? What psychological factors contribute to hypocrisy? These issues will be addressed in chapter 3.

In chapter 4 the closely related issue of moral weakness will be addressed. Is it possible for a person to knowingly act against her better judgment? If so, exactly what is involved in such instances of moral weakness? And how might one successfully avoid such lapses? In chapter 5, the theological doctrines of sin and sanctification will be discussed in order to answer some of these questions.

Chapter 6 will consider the morality of hypocrisy. Is it necessarily a vice? Exactly why is hypocrisy considered morally wrong? And what is it about hypocrisy that makes the trait especially detestable to so many people?

Finally, chapter 7 will consider whether hypocrisy in the church philosophically undermines the Christian worldview, specifically the doctrine that Christians are morally redeemed. If not, then why is there so much hypocrisy in the church?

A Lie Told
by Outward Deeds

Defining Hypocrisy

Where there is no religion, hypocrisy becomes good taste.
George Bernard Shaw

Superstition, idolatry, and hypocrisy have ample wages. But truth goes a-begging.

Martin Luther

Important thinkers have generally agreed that hypocrisy involves some sort of inconsistency involving human behavior. Proceeding with this assumption, we may now ask, What kinds of inconsistencies do we encounter in human affairs? Answering this question can help us further explore the concept of hypocrisy and develop a definition of the term.

EXAMPLES OF INCONSISTENCIES IN HUMAN AFFAIRS

Consider the following case studies.

Case 1. Alice believes racism is a moral outrage and is convinced that it is never acceptable to discriminate against persons on the basis of their ethnicity or skin color. She is appalled by such things as the history of slavery in America and the Nazi holocaust. Precisely because of these injustices, she resents all American Caucasians and Germans. She privately condemns them all as racists.

Case 2. Boris is applying for a job as a regional sales representative for a pet food company. Applicants must have earned a college degree, which, unfortunately, Boris has yet to do. But since he is qualified in all other respects and is only a few hours short of having his degree, Boris misrepresents the facts, both in his resume and during his formal job interview, where he testifies that he has a bachelor's degree.

Case 3. Clark loves the taste of Scotch and the feeling it gives him. However, he is fully persuaded that it is wrong for him to drink liquor, because of his propensity to abuse alcohol. Yet when the opportunity to drink Scotch presents itself, Clark usually splurges. In the morning, upon recalling his actions the previous night, he invariably chides himself and resolves never to give in to the temptation again. Clark has an identical twin, Chris, who shares the love for Scotch and a similar tendency toward abuse as well as the moral conviction that it is wrong for him to indulge because of this tendency. He differs from his brother, however, in that he feels neither regret nor pangs of guilt after drinking large quantities of Scotch.

Case 4. Derek is a politically interested young person who says he is committed to the moral, social, and political agenda of the Libertarian party. He claims to endorse a laissez-faire economic philosophy and only the barest restrictions on personal lifestyle choices, insisting that "it is not the government's place to infringe upon personal autonomy except in those cases in which such restrictions clearly enhance the liberties of others." Yet Derek confesses support for motorcycle helmet laws, saying that "these regulations are in the best interest of cyclists."

Case 5. Erin is an avowed vegetarian for moral reasons, based on her conviction that animals have rights and that livestock farming violates these rights because it is cruel and inhumane. She is outspoken about her beliefs and often publicly lobbies for stricter regulations for animal farming. She strongly advises others to stop eating meat altogether out of respect for the rights of animals. Yet in spite of her convictions, Erin occasionally sneaks hamburgers at fast food restaurants, savoring them for their flavor.

Case 6. Fran, the chief executive officer of a large, well-known corporation, is running for public office. Publicly her behavior is upbeat and positive. During lectures and interviews she typically displays a cheerful and relaxed attitude. She is patient with questioners, deflects criticisms, and successfully resists the temptation to get drawn into the baiting remarks of hagglers. Outside the public eye, however, Fran is rigidly stern with her employees, impatient, tempestuous, and given to harsh personal attacks on those who question her corporate decisions.

A TAXONOMY OF INCONSISTENCIES

These cases differ from one another insofar as some involve overt action (cases 3, 5, and 6) while others do not. As our historical survey would suggest, only those cases that involve outward behavior would ordinarily be described as hypocrisy. Chris, Erin, and Fran are hypocrites, while the others are not. Alice, Boris, Clark, and Derek are guilty of serious inconsistencies, but none of these cases involves the sort of "play-acting" that characterizes hypocrisy (at least based on the data in the scenarios). To work out a rigorous account of hypocrisy, we must arrive at a definition that will apply to all and only genuine instances of the vice. The problem is that while the hypocrite always displays an inconsistency, this may take different forms, depending on what one's behavior is inconsistent with.

Just what variants of hypocrisy are there? Consider three distinct domains of human experience—the behavioral, linguistic, and cognitive. In the cognitive domain, we entertain ideas and develop beliefs. Linguistically, we confess these convictions via the spoken and written word. And behaviorally, our actions express our actual commitments. As the saying goes, "a tree is known by its fruits." Human beings, then, at least implicitly, make truth claims in three basic ways: thought, word, and deed.

None of us maintains perfect harmony among these three dimensions of experience. Such conflicts take various forms, some of which qualify as instances of hypocrisy. Using this threefold distinction between the cognitive, linguistic, and behavioral domains, we can identify six categories of inconsistencies:

Types of Conflict				Associated Problems
1. Cognitive	<——>	Cognitive	=	Cognitive disparity
2. Cognitive	<——>	Linguistic	=	Deception, lying
3. Cognitive	<——>	Behavioral	=	Hypocrisy or moral weakness
4. Linguistic	<——>	Linguistic	=	Verbal inconsistency
5. Linguistic	<——>	Behavioral	=	Hypocrisy or moral weakness
6. Behavioral	<——>	Behavioral	=	Hypocrisy or moral weakness

This characterization of the "problems" associated with each form of inconsistency is only preliminary. Such categorizing is not always so easy. But this schema should at least be useful in organizing our thinking about hypocrisy and related issues.

The six case studies correspond to the six basic forms of conflict identified in the chart. Alice's inconsistency is purely cognitive. She holds logically contradictory beliefs; she is convinced that racism is wrong, yet she harbors antipathy for Germans and American Caucasians. In a word, she is self-deceived. Though self-deception is a complex and controversial phenomenon and some even deny its possibility, we can at least note that if it does exist, it is a form of cognitive disparity.

Boris's case is a typical instance of lying. He knows he has not yet earned a college degree, but he says he has. Whether orally or in writing, he deceives his potential employer. Lying essentially involves a conflict between what one believes to be true and what one confesses as true. An interesting question is whether one's belief must be true in order for one to lie in misrepresenting it. For example, suppose that unknown to him, Boris actually had already satisfied all the requirements for his bachelor's degree, so that his resume was not inaccurate on this matter, nor was his testimony during the interview. If he nonetheless believed that he had yet to earn the degree, would he still be lying? My intuitions, and those of most ethicists, are that Boris would not be lying, since he is, after all, telling the truth. (I am assuming a general definition of lying as false testimony.) But he would be guilty of intention to deceive, which, in this case anyway, is morally blameworthy.

The cases of Clark and Chris might both seem to qualify as hypocrisy, as their firm convictions and resolute intentions are in both cases overcome by the strength of the temptation. But there is a morally relevant difference between the actions of these brothers, since Clark experiences deep remorse afterward and Chris does not. For this reason, Clark is better described as morally weak than as a hypocrite.

Derek's inconsistency, going merely on the data in the scenario, may not be hypocrisy but rather a simple verbal inconsistency. He is apparently unaware that his advocating both libertarian political principles and paternalistic motorcycle helmet laws is logically inconsistent. Of course, if he acts on either of these convictions, he may become guilty of hypocrisy. It would not be the same sort of hypocrisy as that displayed by Chris, but more like that of Erin.

Erin's is a classic example of not practicing what one preaches. She boldly proclaims that eating meat is a moral vice, but she eats meat anyway. There are no extenuating circumstances which might justify her actions. It is out of mere appetite that Erin transgresses what she conceives to be a bona fide moral obligation.

Finally, Fran's behavior in public and in private is so inconsistent that she seems like two different people. Since her spiteful actions predominate when she is out of the public eye, her virtuous behavior is nothing more than a front calculated to create a positive image, an image that does not reflect the "real" Fran.

Of these six kinds of inconsistency, three involve action. Minimally, then, it seems that a hypocrite is one who acts inconsistently with her beliefs, words, or other actions. This definition, based on the above taxonomy of inconsistencies, suggests three kinds of hypocrisy:

A cognitive-behavioral hypocrite is someone who believes X and yet acts inconsistently with this conviction.

A linguistic-behavioral hypocrite is someone who confesses X and yet acts inconsistently with this confession.

A behavioral-behavioral hypocrite is someone whose actions are inconsistent with one another.

The vice of hypocrisy, whichever of these three forms it takes, might be seen as roughly analogous to logical inconsistency. Two propositions are said to be inconsistent or contradictory if both cannot be simultaneously affirmed. To affirm contradictory propositions is the very essence of irrationality. Similarly, the hypocrite engages in actions which, as it were, contradict or "negate" one another morally. One is morally good, while the other is bad. Thus, the hypocrite is irrational, because inconsistent, in the moral sense.

FOUR SPECIES OF HYPOCRISY

This threefold distinction is but one of several possible ways of organizing brands of hypocrisy. In one of the more illuminating recent discussions of the topic, Roger Crisp and Christopher Cowton offer a fourfold distinction of the vice: hypocrisies of pretense, blame, inconsistency, and complacency.[1]

The hypocrisy of pretense occurs when a person puts up a front of being morally better than he is. They identify Moliere's Tartuffe as a vivid example of this kind of hypocrisy. The Pharisees in the New Testament are another example. It is this species of the vice that Jesus condemns in the following passage: "When you pray, do not be like the hypocrites, for they love to pray standing in the synagogues and on the street corners to be seen by men. I tell you the truth, they have received their reward in full. But when you pray, go into your room, close the door and pray to your Father, who is unseen."[2]

Like Tartuffe, the New Testament Pharisees are pretentious hypocrites, motivated by desire for selfish gain. But as Crisp and Cowton note, this need not always be the case. Pretenses may be motivated by malice,[3] shame,[4] and even interest in others.[5] Nor must the pretense aim to sham genuine virtue.[6]

Another species is the hypocrisy of blame, defined by Crisp and Cowton as "moral criticism of others by someone with moral faults of their own."[7] The televangelist who castigates the sexually impure, while he himself is a habitual sexual offender, provides a graphic example, as does the cocaine-addict politician who condemns drug dealers. Although the most despicable instances of wrongful blaming regard those who condemn others for vices of which they are themselves guilty, this is not a requirement for the hypocrisy of blame. As Crisp and Cowton argue, "the vice often appears to lie particularly in the fact that the fault of the critic is worse than that criticized."[8] In the Sermon on the Mount, it is the hypocrisy of blame that Jesus is exposing when he says, "How can you say to your brother, 'Let me take the speck out of your eye,' when all the time there is a plank in your own eye? You hypocrite, first take the plank out of your own eye, and then you will see clearly to remove the speck from your brother's eye."[9] And King David's response to the prophet Nathan's parable provides a striking example of the hypocrisy of blame. David's response of condemnation for the man in the parable was inconsistent with the fact that he was guilty of an even greater sin.[10]

The third category of hypocrisy identified by Crisp and Cowton is that of inconsistency, which they define as "the uttering of some (overriding) moral requirement that does apply to oneself and then failing to live up to it."[11] This instance of the vice is evidenced in the well-known phrase "Do as I say, not as I do."

It is this sort of hypocrisy that Judith Sklar regards as "the distance between assertion and performance."[12] In recent years American politicians have been increasingly criticized for this sort of hypocrisy, as many have preached commitment to higher ethical standards but in practice have themselves fallen far short of their avowed ideals. Saul's consulting the witch of Endor after publicly condemning spiritism falls into this category.[13]

Lastly, Crisp and Cowton identify complacency in certain conditions as a form of hypocrisy. To be guilty of this is to ignore the demands of morality when they become costly, to be content with one's moral status, refusing to improve or even to reflect upon it, while carrying on a pretense of virtue, blaming others for their vices, or failing to practice what one preaches. Thus, as Crisp and Cowton note, complacent hypocrites protect "their complacency from criticism on the grounds of the first three kinds of hypocrisy."[14]

Jesus' diatribe in Matthew 23 best illustrates the essence of this form of hypocrisy in his most sustained rebuke of the Pharisees:

> Woe to you, teachers of the law and Pharisees, you hypocrites! You give a tenth of your spices—mint, dill and cummin. But you have neglected the more important matters of the law—justice, mercy and faithfulness. You should have practiced the latter, without neglecting the former. You blind guides! You strain out a gnat but swallow a camel. . . .
>
> Woe to you, teachers of the law and Pharisees, you hypocrites! You are like whitewashed tombs, which look beautiful on the outside but on the inside are full of dead men's bones and everything unclean. In the same way, on the outside you appear to people as righteous but on the inside you are full of hypocrisy and wickedness.[15]

Crisp and Cowton's fourfold analysis of hypocrisy is very helpful. But does their account fit with the taxonomy presented earlier? I think so.

Without making a detailed justification for the following claims, I would propose that the hypocrisies of pretense are generally of the behavioral-behavioral kind. Instances of the hypocrisy of blame fall into the linguistic-behavioral category, as they always involve an inconsistency between one's moral claims (which happen to take the form of a verbal rebuke or condemnation) and one's actions. The hypocrisy of inconsistency, at least as defined by Crisp and Cowton, is of the behavioral-behavioral type. But I see no reason why their definition may not be broadened to include other kinds of inconsistencies as well, so that the inconsistent hypocrite may fall into any of my three categories. Similarly, instances of the hypocrisy of complacency could also fall into any of these

categories, as suggested by Crisp and Cowton's own assertion that such hypocrites may sustain their complacency
through any of the other forms of hypocrisy—pretense, blame,
or inconsistency.

THE ROOT OF HYPOCRISY

Having formulated a general definition of hypocrisy, the
issue becomes complicated again when we ask in any particular case of hypocritical behavior, Why does the person act
this way? What generates this disparity between one's actions
and one's beliefs, confessions, or other actions? Here writers
on the topic seriously diverge, and it is a challenge to make
sense of their conflicting theories. There are two general ways
of conceiving the root of hypocrisy. Some writers maintain
that hypocrisy, at least in some forms, is rooted in self-deceit.
As was noted in the first chapter, Joseph Butler dubbed the
phenomenon "internal hypocrisy." He discusses this in some
of his sermons, where he explains that when hypocrites "hear
the vice and folly of what is in truth their own course of life,
exposed in the justest and strongest manner, they will often
assent to it, and even carry the matter further; persuading
themselves, one does not know how, but some way or other
persuading themselves that they are out of the case, and that
it hath no relation to them."[16]

In a similar vein, Bela Szabados notes that the hypocrite
may "pay lip service to reason" by "rationalisation, explaining away the evidence unfavourable to one's belief, trying to
make one's position appear reasonable."[17] If these observa-
tions are accurate, the self-deceived or "internal" hypocrite is
characterized by a psyche fractured by a refusal to fully own
up to some moral truth she knows in her heart of hearts.

We might be inclined to flippantly label such persons delusional, but as Raphael Demos observes, there is an important
distinction to be made between delusion and self-deceit. The
former involves total belief, whereas the latter is a kind of
"make believe" in which one pretends to believe what she
knows is not the case.[18] The delusional person experiences
no conflict in her belief of a lie, for she is completely con-

vinced. The self-deceived, on the other hand, does experience conflict because her belief contradicts her knowledge.

For instance, suppose that Chris, in case study 3, justifies his drinking by telling himself that he is not drunk, because he is not "out of control" during his bender. Although fully convinced that it is morally wrong for him to get drunk and also knowing full well the feeling of this physical and psychological state, he attempts to persuade himself that he is not presently drunk by altering the definition, at least for the time being. Chris is self-deceived, and his self-deceit gives rise to his hypocrisy.

Or take the case of Erin, who lobbies for animal rights and protests against cattle, pig, and chicken farming. She justifies her foray into a hamburger joint with this reasoning: "I am hungry and tired. This fast-food place is not only convenient; it's cheap. Anyway, I have worked hard for the rights of animals, probably improving the overall quality of life for livestock. One hamburger is not going to make much difference and almost certainly won't hurt our cause." In this way Erin tries to convince herself that her actions are morally inconsequential.

Finally, consider Fran's duplicitous behavior. In public she is all cordiality and smiles. But away from the camera's eye she is sardonic and rude, belittling all those around her. She justifies her inconsiderate behavior in the name of expediency, reasoning that it is the most effective way to motivate others to work their hardest to achieve success in the world of politics. "Nice gals finish last," she reminds herself and then proceeds to blister members of her staff with insults.

Thus, we see how self-deception can give rise to hypocrisy. In such cases, hypocrisy is clearly a moral vice. But some writers prefer to see hypocrisy as a "second-order" or "meta" vice. In the words of Crisp and Cowton, it is symptomatic of "a failure to take morality seriously."[19] We might say that it is metavirtuous to choose to acknowledge the domain of morality, that is, to be a moralist.[20] But the hypocrite is metavicious, for she tacitly refuses to do so, and is therefore an amoralist. Such a person considers herself somehow exempt from moral constraints. And yet, being aware of how the moral community operates and when and why rewards are doled out to the virtuous, the hypocrite plays a part for personal gain.[21] As Christine McKinnon notes, the hypocrite "wishes a certain status and she recognizes that this can be achieved if she can manage to elicit positive moral assessments."[22] So like the self-deceived hypocrite, the amoralist hypocrite gains praise and respect for qualities she does not really possess. But unlike the self-deceived hypocrite, she experiences no psychological dissonance, because she is genuinely convinced that she is not subject to the relevant moral rules.

Returning to the cases of Chris, Erin, and Fran, we might describe their behavior in terms of the failure to take morality seriously. In each of these cases the person in question could be seen as simply disregarding the call of morality on his or her own life. Chris affirms the general moral duty to sobriety in the abstract but refuses to apply it to his own life. Similarly, Erin and Fran generally affirm the values of respect for animals and humans respectively but somehow see themselves as exempt from these obligations.

Now the question is just how different is this lack of moral seriousness from self-deception? In one respect they are not very different at all. In fact, lack of moral seriousness can be construed as a species of self-deception. So there is a difference here, but as I will explain, it is a difference in degree, not kind. Both are forms of self-deception, and both are self-deceptions of a moral sort.

The distinction here is between what we may call "local" and "global" moral self-deception. Local moral self-deception involves justifying one's inconsistency by maintaining that an act one performs is an exception to the moral law, a moral law that one affirms. This is self-deception about the morality of a particular act or habit, as one persuades herself that it is legitimate when she knows deep down that the act is wrong. Global moral self-deception, on the other hand, involves justifying one's inconsistency by rejecting the moral law itself. This is amoralism, in which one attempts to see herself as outside the whole moral community, when in fact she knows that she cannot escape it (hence her attempts to appear righteous). This is self-deception about one's very relationship to the realm of morality. Thus we could say that all hypocrisy is caused by self-deception, but only if we broaden the concept to include global moral self-deception, that is, self-deception about morality itself.

So we can conceive of one and the same hypocrite's actions as resulting from self-deceit or lack of moral seriousness. Both accounts of the cause of hypocrisy have something to recommend them. Each has explanatory power, yet neither is likely to be adequate as a total explanation for all cases of hypocrisy. For this reason I prefer to regard self-deceit and amoralism as dual causes of hypocritical behavior. This is to say, each of them may be a sufficient but neither of them a necessary condition for hypocrisy. So what I propose is a disjunctive definition of the root of hypocrisy: it is a conflict or disparity between apparent and actual righteousness resulting from moral self-deceit *or* a lack of moral seriousness.

Hypocrisy: Vice and Metavice?

As we have seen, hypocrisy may be variously deemed a first-order moral vice (self-deceit) or a metavice (lack of moral seriousness). A natural presumption made by some who discuss hypocrisy is that it need always be one or the other. But why? As Aristotle cautions those who dare to inquire into ethical matters, "We must not expect more precision than the subject matter admits."[23] The aim of devising a unified and coherent theory of hypocrisy is reasonable, but we must not allow this goal to blind us to the real complexity of the phenomenon. Anyway, the fact that hypocrisy is on different occasions a first-order or second-order vice helps to account for the difficulties the subject has posed for moral philosophers.

Hypocrisy as a metavice is but a symptom of amorality, a tacit declaration of one's rejection of the call to the moral life. This, of course, is to be distinguished from other cases of amoralism such as that found in Nietzsche, who declared openly the specter of nihilism and called for a "transvaluation of values."[24] With hypocrisy, one's amoralism becomes apparent through behavior. Our (the moralists') annoyance at this is at least as great as that prompted by self-confessed amoralists such as Nietzsche, probably because of the hypocrite's attempt at deception. In either case, to be guilty of the meta-vice of amoralism does not exempt one from being guilty of first-order vice as well. For if there is indeed a moral law, denying its existence does not free one from the moral de-mands on one's life any more than denying the law of grav-ity will keep one from falling.

When hypocrisy is a first-order vice, what is the cause of this self-deceit? Why does the self-deceived hypocrite fail to see the inconsistency in her life? As mentioned earlier, Butler suggests that this results from either self-ignorance or self-absorption.[25] In the former case, one fails to adequately eval-uate one's own actions by the same standards one uses to evaluate others or to thoroughly evaluate all of one's actions by the moral law. In the latter, one is preoccupied with one-self and one's immediate interests to the extent that he doesn't bother to compare them with those of others which he con-demns. To the extent that a person inclines toward either self-ignorance or self-absorption, he is prone to fall into hypocrisy. The ideal balance, it would seem, is to be highly self-aware without being self-absorbed.

Christian redemption, then, should be a cure and preven-tative of hypocrisy, as Christians are provided effective means for becoming both more self-aware and less self-absorbed. The Scriptures and the Holy Spirit reveal us to ourselves, mak-ing us aware of the moral standard and showing us our true sinful colors. In this way we are made more self-aware. The Scriptures and Holy Spirit also enlighten our minds and sen-sitize our hearts to the needs and concerns of others, making us less selfish. We thereby become less self-absorbed. Chap-ter 5 will examine more closely this process of moral improve-ment, or sanctification, in the life of the Christian.

HYPOCRISY, AKRASIA, AND POOR MORAL INSIGHT

We have identified one feature common to all cases of hypocrisy, namely, a disparity involving conduct. But this alone is not a sufficient condition for hypocrisy, for there are clear cases of persons whose actions are not consistent with their beliefs, words, or other actions who are not properly regarded as hypocrites. Consider, for example, Clark in case study 3. Like Chris, he succumbs to the temptation to drink Scotch, but unlike his brother he experiences deep anguish over his failure to act consistently with his convictions. His sorrow moves him to repent of his actions yet again, although further failures likely await him. Such a person is not properly regarded as a hypocrite but rather as a sufferer from *akrasia* (moral weakness). The paradigm biblical case of weakness of will is Peter's denial of Christ. The impetuous disciple confidently guaranteed Jesus that he would not deny him, even if all the others did. Jesus, of course, declared Peter's proclamation false. After his three denials when the cock crowed, Peter was reminded of this and wept bitterly. Part of the explanation for Peter's actions lies in the trauma of the moment, specifically the prospect of Peter's own arrest and punishment. His denials did not result from self-deceit or lack of moral seriousness. Rather, Peter's sin resulted from *akrasia.*

Scholars have struggled to fully characterize the *akrates* and to clearly distinguish such a person from the hypocrite. Two elements seem to distinguish *akrasia* from hypocrisy. First, the *akrates* is sincerely committed to the moral standards she professes. She takes morality seriously. Second, the *akrates* experiences genuine remorse after her act. These factors are not the essence of *akrasia* so much as they are signs of it. They signify a weak will or lack of self-control (as opposed to self-deception or lack of moral seriousness).

The objection may be raised, "How can we be sure that such a person really takes morality seriously? After all, doesn't his transgression betray his lack of concern for moral living?" But such an approach faces two serious problems. First, it does not square with some of the plain facts of the moral life, namely, the common experience of giving in to pressure or simply lacking the strength to resist a temptation one sincerely hoped to overcome.[26] Second, and more fundamental, this view would imply that all failures to live up to one's moral ideals are cases of hypocrisy, which in turn implies that all moralists are hypocrites (since all fail morally at one time or another) and all sins are sins of hypocrisy. This is obviously false; otherwise hypocrites would not be singled out as a special breed of sinners.

Is it possible to know just when the inconsistency between one's behavior and one's apparent moral commitments is due to moral weakness and when it suggests genuine hypocrisy? After all, the *akrates* and the hypocrite are *prima facie* identical.[27] This is indeed a problem, but it is essentially an epistemological one. Yes, it is difficult at times to decipher whether a given immoral act constitutes hypocritical behavior or if it is the result of a weak will. Typically, however, there are enough contextual clues in a given situation to provide sufficient evidence to conclude one way or the other. The strength of the temptation is one important consideration, as in the case of Clark's indulgence in liquor. This might be a mitigating circumstance that helps us reconcile his moral commitment with his vice. We do not extend this benefit of the doubt to Chris, as he shows no remorse after his binge. Nor do we attribute Erin's carnivorous behavior to *akrasia,* because we do not consider her temptation to eat meat sufficiently strong.

To return to our biblical examples, in Peter's denial of Christ we find strong mitigating circumstances in the prospect of his arrest and punishment, whereas, in the case of the Pharisees, we see only the will to appear more righteous than they are. Finally, the case of Saul and the witch of Endor is somewhat less clear cut. Admittedly, Saul was genuinely tempted to use a medium, but it seems his action would be much more easily avoided than Peter's. Perhaps what this suggests is that the line between hypocrisy and *akrasia* is not a sharp one. In fact, these two traits might represent ends of a continuum, so that we might say that one is more or less a hypocrite and more or less an *akrates.*

Another phenomenon that could be confused with hypocrisy is immoral behavior resulting from poor moral insight. Suppose Derek, in case study 4, decided to actively campaign for motorcycle helmet laws in spite of his avowed libertarian ideals. Though some might label him a hypocrite, in fact this is not so much a case of hypocrisy as it is one of poor ethical judgment. His pro-paternalist campaigning is consistent with his particular conviction about highway safety, but since it is inconsistent with his broader conviction about libertarian political ideals, the appearance of hypocrisy is unavoidable. Note the difference between Derek and the cognitive-behavioral hypocrite. If Derek possessed better reasoning skills, he would bring his behavior into line. Such is not the case with the cognitive-behavioral hypocrite, who persists in her behavior in spite of her awareness of moral values to the contrary.

So there are crucial distinctions to be made between the hypocrite, the *akrates,* and the person of poor moral insight. In the words of Piers Benn, "hypocrites are generally regarded as insincere in their professed adherence to their principles, whereas the faults of the other two characters are quite different. The sufferer of *akrasia* is not insincere but weak, and the other character has a genuine desire to do what is right, but lacks the necessary inferential powers to see what is right."[28]

THE SOCIAL BENEFITS OF HYPOCRISY

Hypocrisy is sometimes denounced as the worst of all vices because it represents a lack of integrity and even undermines morality itself. Yet one may ask whether there is some bright side to this moral blight. Does hypocrisy have any social benefits? I believe there are potentially at least three distinct benefits of hypocrisy, two direct and one indirect.

First, it may be argued that the pretentious hypocrite can have a positive effect by modeling certain virtues. If we assume that one's performance of a virtuous act makes a constructive contribution to the moral community, it seems reasonable to conclude that the hypocrite's fraudulent behavior may have moral benefits, so long as her inconsistency is not found out. As Piers Benn notes, "appearances are all-important, since they wield a sanction which is conducive to moderation and discretion—even if not perfection—in private conduct."[29]

Second, hypocrites may positively affect others by the preaching they do not practice. Again, Benn argues in this connection that "just as an evil-doer who leads others astray might be thought much worse than an evil-doer who does not try to influence others, so (one would think), a wrong-doer who leads others to do good (by his hypocritical, but perhaps persuasive preaching) is rather better than a wrong-doer who has no beneficial influence upon others. There is no reason why we should not listen to hypocrites (depending of course on what they say); the important thing is (normally) not to imitate them."[30]

Presumably, many of us who take morality seriously and who are successfully duped by the moral impostors among us are actually edified by their exhortations to virtue. This is admittedly a good thing, and to this extent the effects of hypocrisy are beneficial.

A third benefit is indirect. We are all aware of the outrage public hypocrisies inspire. In the gospels, Jesus is most vehement when condemning the Pharisees for this vice. Most people resonate with these sentiments, and such antipathy toward hypocritical behavior in turn stimulates deeper moral circumspection for the rest of us. The ugliness of exposed hypocrisy is a tremendous incentive to avoid falling into it, if for no other reason but to save ourselves the embarrassment of public ridicule.

Thus, it seems the hypocrite, when successful at her masquerade, may sometimes make a positive contribution to society by reinforcing virtuous living. Hypocrisy has been called "the tribute that vice pays to virtue," for the hypocrite shows respect for moral standards at least insofar as she works to appear to abide by them. Every counterfeit implies significant worth in that which it imitates. Hypocrisy is no exception.

In spite of the potential social benefits of hypocrisy, it remains a vice. Or does it? Eighteenth-century philosopher Bernard Mandeville in his *Fable of the Bees* defended the notion that "private vices bring public benefits." Nor would classical utilitarians, who define moral goodness solely in terms of the consequences of actions, be able to rule out the possibility of the moral legitimacy of certain forms of hypocrisy, precisely because of the social utility of the trait. One's answers to the questions whether and why hypocrisy is a moral vice may depend, then, upon one's moral theory. In chapter 6 we will analyze hypocrisy in the light of various moral theories.

THE HYPOCRITE AND THE IRONIC PERSON

What of hypocrisy's mirror opposite, the trait of acting or pretending to be less pious than one actually is? The person who does this is ironic, which is hardly a vicious characteristic. On the contrary, the ironic figure plays a constructive moral role, intending her masquerade to be penetrated. In the words of Christine McKinnon, "the ironical person pretends to be worse, not better, than she is, according to accepted standards, and she intends to be unmasked, so as to expose the inadequacies of these same standards."[31]

The philosopher Socrates is the epitome of the ironic figure. Upon hearing of the Delphic oracle's pronouncement that he was the wisest among men, Socrates is incredulous: "I said to myself, What does the god mean? Why does he not use plain language? I am only too conscious that I have no claim to wisdom, great or small. So what can he mean by asserting that I am the wisest man in the world?"[32]

Thus, the most famous philosopher in Western history set out to disprove the Oracle's proclamation, only to find that the testimony was true. Socrates, unlike his fellow Athenians, at least recognized how little he really knew, and to this extent he was wiser than the rest.

Was Socrates sincere in his humility? Did his confession that "all I know is that I know nothing" reflect his truest convictions? Perhaps this is a moot issue, the main point being his intent to reveal to the Athenians just how morally misguided they were, that theirs were false standards of piety which exalted the pompous and proud rather than the truly wise and virtuous.

Jesus, too, was an ironic figure in the Socratic tradition.[33] Like the leaders at Athens four centuries earlier, the Pharisees were popularly regarded as paragons of wisdom. The appearance of the humble Galilean proved to be their undoing. Jesus' irony served a purpose similar to that of Socrates: to expose the moral corruption of the religious elite of his day. Of course, in the latter case the irony is immeasurably more profound, as Jesus was not only most wise among men but divine. The moral lesson is unmistakable, as Paul highlights in Philippians: "Your attitude should be the same as that of Christ Jesus: Who, being in very nature God, did not consider equality with God something to be grasped, but made himself nothing, taking the very nature of a servant, being made in human likeness."[34]

It seems, then, that the ironic figure is the moral polar opposite of the hypocrite. The latter is a moral freeloader, deceiving others to gain undeserved praise. The former creates the illusion of being less virtuous than she really is, for the sake of inspiring others to moral goodness and exposing hypocrisy itself. Perhaps the reason hypocrisy is looked upon with such disdain is that (at least in some forms) it is directly antithetical to humility, an essential Christian virtue.

CONCLUSION

Hypocrisy is a kind of inconsistency in human life which always involves behavior of some sort. Specifically, a hypocrite is one who acts inconsistently with her beliefs, words, or other actions, due to either self-deception or lack of moral seriousness. So it is in some cases a simple moral vice and in other cases a second-order moral vice. Hypocrisy is not to be confused with moral weakness or poor moral insight. Nor should the actions of the ironical figure be thought hypocritical, for she intends her sham to be revealed for morally and socially constructive purposes. Finally, in spite of the fact that hypocrisy is a morally vicious trait, it does provide some social benefits such as reinforcing ethical ideals and, when exposed, prompting persons to deeper moral circumspection.

Taking Oneself In

Self-Deception

Facts do not cease to exist because they are ignored.
Aldous Huxley

Make it thy business to know thyself, which is the most difficult lesson in the world.
Cervantes

We have seen that hypocrisy may take one of two forms. It may be a first-order vice, in which case the hypocrite is self-deceived. Or it may be a second-order vice, a failure to take morality itself seriously. Just what it means to lack moral seriousness is fairly straightforward. Such a person is a moral nihilist. He denies the existence of a moral law or rejects the notion that it applies to him. His behavior becomes hypocritical when he makes a pretense (by word or deed) of being one who affirms the existence of moral absolutes. Hypocrisy as a first-order vice, however, is not nearly so easily analyzed. The concept of self-deception is a tricky one and has been a source

44

of much philosophical controversy in recent decades. In this chapter we will look at several models of self-deception.

THE PARADOX OF SELF-DECEPTION AND FOUR STRATEGIES TO SOLVE IT

People who are self-deceived seem to deny or disbelieve what they know to be true. Consider the loyal mother who persists in believing that her son is "really a good boy" even though he has been arrested repeatedly for assorted crimes. While her son's true moral colors should be clear to her, she nevertheless affirms his essential goodness. How do we explain such cases?

The problem facing philosophers and psychologists as they attempt to do so concerns the following paradox: In cases of self-deception the subject knows X and denies (disbelieves) X. Since knowledge of X implies belief in the truth of X, it seems that the self-deceived must both believe and disbelieve X. But this is a plain contradiction. How are we to resolve this paradox?[1]

Since 1960 there has been much discussion of self-deception, and numerous attempts have been made to solve the paradox. In my review of the vast literature on the topic, I have found four basic approaches to the problem.[2] First, there are "partitioning" strategies, which see self-deception as analogous to interpersonal deception and appeal to divisions or "partitions" within a single mind to explain self-deception. Second, there are "epistemic" approaches, which reject the interpersonal model and assume a unified view of the self. This strategy prefers to see self-deception as basically a form of irrational belief. Third, there are "moderate" strategies, which incorporate elements of the first two views, proposing a limited partitioning of the self and recognizing a degree of irrationality in self-deception. Moderate strategies also tend to assume an interpersonal model of self-deception. Finally, there is the "existential" approach, which rejects the assumption of the first three views that self-deception is cognitive. Rather, the existential strategy sees the phenomenon as volitional: the self-deceiver simply disavows some activity in which he or she is involved.

45

Partitioning Strategies

Self-Deception as Lying to Oneself

The most famous twentieth century philosophical discussion of self-deception comes from the existentialist Jean Paul Sartre. In his monumental *Being and Nothingness* he exposits the notion of *mauvaise foi* or "bad faith." "The one who practices bad faith," he says, "is hiding a displeasing truth or presenting as truth a pleasing untruth."[3] So, according to Sartre, bad faith is a lie told to oneself. What distinguishes bad faith from ordinary lying, of course, is that it involves deception not of another but of oneself. As Sartre explains, in bad faith "the one to whom the lie is told and the one who lies are one and the same person, which means that I must know in my capacity as deceiver the truth which is hidden from me in my capacity as the one deceived. Better yet I must know the truth very exactly *in order* to conceal it more carefully."[4]

When so stated, the phenomenon of bad faith seems strange indeed. How can the deceived also be the deceiver? Sartre provides an illuminating example to make sense of this paradox. Consider a woman who agrees to go on a date with a man in whom she is not romantically interested. They visit a restaurant and begin to enjoy a pleasant dining experience together. But then, he takes her hand. At this point the woman faces a dilemma.

> To leave the hand there is to consent in herself to flirt, to engage herself. To withdraw it is to break the troubled and unstable harmony which gives the hour its charm. The aim is to postpone the moment of decision as long as possible. We know what happens next; the young woman leaves her hand there, but she *does not notice* that she is leaving it. She does not notice because it happens by chance that she is at this moment all intellect. She draws her companion up to the most lofty regions of sentimental speculation; she speaks of Life, of her life, she shows herself in her essential aspect—a personality, a consciousness. And during this time the divorce of the body from the soul is accomplished; the hand rests inert between the warm hands of her companion—neither consenting nor resisting—a thing.[5]

Thus, the woman self-deceives by pretending not to notice. She even distracts and preoccupies herself by "intellectualizing" an emotionally pregnant situation, a process with which we are all familiar. This is but one instance of the basic pattern of bad faith, according to Sartre—lying to oneself.

Much more could be said about Sartre's analysis, but a complete appraisal would take us deep into the technical details of his metaphysics. Nor is it necessary, since similar models have been proposed independently of complex metaphysical systems. In 1960, for instance, Raphael Demos published an article defending a roughly Sartrian account of self-deception, which similarly models the phenomenon on the concept of lying to others. This article sparked intense debate on the subject of self-deception which lasted throughout the sixties.[6] Demos begins with the following analysis of lying:

The expression "B lies to (deceives) C" means:

1. B intends to induce a mistaken belief in C.
2. B succeeds in carrying out this intention.
3. B knows that what he tells C is false.[7]

In Demos's view, then, to self-deceive is to knowingly induce a mistaken belief in oneself. Such a person "persuades himself to believe what he *knows* is not so. In short, self-deception entails that B believes both P and not-P at the same time. Thus self-deception involves an inner conflict, perhaps the existence of a contradiction."[8] Now self-deception, Demos notes, is not to be confused with delusion, in which case the person "experiences no conflict," unlike the self-deceived person.

Demos's model illustrates what was earlier described as the paradox of self-deception: how can we account for the persistence of belief in two contrary propositions? Or how can a person really believe what he knows is not true? The peculiar nature of self-deception is acknowledged even by lay persons who scratch their heads over persons who believe something to be true although they "know better." The challenge to Demos's model, or to any theory of self-deception for that matter, is to resolve this apparent logical contradiction while at the same time preserving the very real "inner conflict" that characterizes self-deception.

Reminiscent of Sartre, Demos solves this problem by appealing to the concept of "noticing." Just as some feelings can go unnoticed by a person (as when one does not "notice" her headache when engrossed in a great film), so beliefs may go unnoticed. Demos elaborates: "There are two levels of awareness possible; one is simple awareness, the other awareness together with attending, or noticing. It follows that I may be aware of something without, at the same time, noticing or focusing my attention on it."[9]

So, for instance, in the case of the loyal mother, she may persist in her belief in her child's goodness by simply ignoring various reports about his mischief. She refuses to call these facts to her conscious attention, though she truly knows them and the truth about her son that they imply.[10]

Is Demos's model correct? For all its initial plausibility, his view has incurred extensive criticism. Some critics deny that self-deception should even be modeled upon the concept of interpersonal deception.[11] And even if the interpersonal model is sound, a fuller explication of the different levels of awareness is necessary to make Demos's view plausible.

Another criticism of Demos is posed by Herbert Fingarette who argues that Demos's view does not sufficiently distinguish self-deception from simple irrationality (believing a contradiction).[12] He notes that in any case in which a person holds inconsistent beliefs we must ask whether he does so intentionally. If so, the person believes a contradiction, which is paradoxical. If not, he is simply ignorant. To reduce self-deception to a failure to "notice" the inconsistency in one's belief is to oversimplify the phenomenon. It does not do justice to the dimension of "taking oneself in" that characterizes the self-deceived person.

Compartmentalist Theories

There is a cluster of models that attempt to avoid the paradox of self-deception (and overcome the limitations of a Demosian-type approach) by dividing the self in one way or another. This view is sometimes called "compartmentalism," and its most famous exponent is Sigmund Freud, the father of the psychoanalytic school of modern psychology. He proposed a "tripartheid" view of the soul, where each aspect performs distinct, sometimes conflicting, functions. For this reason Freud has frequently been consulted by philosophers of mind striving to work out a satisfactory account of self-deception.

According to Freud, the human personality is made up of an id, ego, and superego. Their corporate purpose is to enable the individual to thrive in her environment, meet basic needs, and fulfill desires. These aspects of the mind may work together harmoniously, in which case the person is psychologically healthy and practically efficient. If conflict prevails, the result is mental sickness and psychopathology.

The id is that aspect of the personality that functions to satisfy what Freud calls the "pleasure principle," an innate drive to experience pleasure and avoid pain. It is indulgent, impulsive, and nonrational, preoccupied with the body and its cravings. The ego, on the other hand, abides by the "reality principle" and seeks to meet the demands of the external world. Its task is to manage and regulate the demands of the id in order to meet actual needs. The third aspect of the psyche is the superego, whose motivating influence is moral and social ideals internalized by the individual in the course of natural development.

Now, in Freud's view, tension between the ideals of the superego and the brute, often unconscious desires of the id naturally and regularly result in internal conflict, and the ego must play the executive role in determining how best to satisfy basic impulses without transgressing social and moral norms. Inevitably, certain of the id's desires must be ignored, unsatisfied, or "repressed."

When Freudian psychology is applied to the phenomenon of self-deception, we get a model that extends the partitioning of consciousness suggested by the theories previously examined. In Freud's view, one may unconsciously know one thing and, due to the impulses of the id, consciously believe something wholly contradictory.[13] That is, the self-deceived person, according to Freud, unconsciously knows X but consciously believes not-X.

Another version of compartmentalism is offered by Amelie Oksenberg Rorty, who likewise denies that the self is a strict unity. Rather, it is more properly conceived as a sort of community, "a loose configuration of habits, habits of thought and perception and motivation and action."[14] Of course, this "loose configuration" must have a governing center or central authority which guides and directs these habits. Thus, says Rorty, the *I* may be conceived in one of two ways, either as (1) the entire system of habits or (2) the central governing authority. And yet it is not always the central authority whose voice is heard when a person speaks. Hence a person's ability "to believe what one knows is not true." Self-deception, then, according to Rorty, is simply a state of "deep division" within the self, occurring as a result of conflict between various aspects of the self "community."[15]

David Pears proposes a more elaborate compartmentalism in his book *Motivated Irrationality*.[16] He defends what he calls a "functional" theory of mental subsystems. One's conscious beliefs are formed by his main mental system. But information processed in one's mind may be affected by beliefs of certain "subsystems" of the mind. One example of such subsystem beliefs are "cautionary beliefs," which are beliefs, for example, that "given the evidence it would be irrational to believe P." Pears notes that in one's main mental system "there is a schism whenever there is irrationality that the person is competent to avoid. . . . For if someone is competent to avoid a piece of irrationality, the cautionary belief will be somewhere within him, and, if it does not intervene and stop the irrationality, it will be assigned to a sub-system."[17]

Such assignment of beliefs to subsystems, Pears suggests, is done automatically by the mind so it may maintain normal function.[18] Take, for example, a self-proclaimed "ladies' man," who persists in pursuing a woman who resists his every romantic overture. Rather than acknowledging the obvious meaning of the evidence (e.g., she refuses invitations to dinner, avoids him at the office, sneers at his compliments, etc.), he grows more confident that she is genuinely interested, bolstered by his belief that she is "playing hard to get."

How would compartmentalists explain this? The Freudian would appeal to the man's repressed desire for sexual gratification which has produced a conviction about the woman's desires. His lust for her is so strong that the resulting pressure upon the ego must be relieved by "projecting" upon her the same desires he has. Similarly, Rorty would explain the man's persistence in terms of his deeply divided mind. While aspects of his mind might acknowledge her signals for what they are, the desires or habits of other parts of his self "community" would manifest themselves more strongly.[19] Pears's interpretation would be that the man actually has the belief that his confidence is irrational, but it has been relegated to a subsystem whose affect on his main mental system has been blocked by a strong desire for the woman.

Serious problems face the compartmentalist theory of self-deception. One traditional criticism of Freudian psychology in particular focuses on the notion of an unconscious mind. Specifically, how are we to conceive of unconscious knowledge? If knowledge presupposes belief and belief implies awareness, then it would seem that to have knowledge demands consciousness. But then the whole notion of "unconscious knowledge" appears self-contradictory.[20] This is hardly a satisfying resolution to the paradox of self-deception.

A Pearsian brand of compartmentalism faces similar difficulties or "psychological puzzles," as Mark Johnston notes:

> How could the deceiving subsystem have the capacities required to perpetrate the deception? . . . Why should the deceiving subsystem be interested in the deception? Does it like lying for its own sake? Or does it suppose that it knows what is best for the deceived system to believe?
>
> Again, how does the deceiving system engage in an extended campaign of deception, employing various stratagems to alter the beliefs of the deceived system, without the deceived system's somehow noticing? If the deceived system somehow notices then the deception cannot succeed without the collusion of the deceived system. However, to speak of the collusion of the deceived system in its own deception simply reintroduces the original problem.[21]

The original problem to which Johnston alludes is, of course, the paradox of self-deception.

Another criticism which may be applied to compartmentalist accounts in general is suggested by Stanley Paluch.[22] He argues that this approach neglects an important aspect of self-deception. First, note that in any case of interpersonal deception the deceiver has the capacity to "undeceive" his victim and refuses to do so. Similarly, in cases of self-deception, the person can undeceive himself but does not. However, in a compartmentalist view there is this crucial difference between the two forms of deception. In the case of self-deception, the person is not aware of his capacity to undeceive himself. For to be unconscious is to be unaware. But then, if Freud is right, it seems that the self-deceived person does not have a genuine capacity to undeceive himself after all. For, as Paluch notes, "to assign me a capacity is to imply that I could realize that capacity under the appropriate circumstances."[23] But the self-deceived person could never realize that capacity, since he is necessarily unaware of it, so he really does not have this capacity at all. The compartmentalist model, then, is incoherent.

EPISTEMIC STRATEGIES

An alternate approach rejects the interpersonal model of self-deception and prefers to interpret the phenomenon as a special case of irrationality, in which the self-deceived stubbornly maintains an unwarranted belief. Like compartmentalist theories, this "epistemic" approach rejects the notion that self-deception is paradoxical.

One such account is proposed by John Canfield and Don Gustavson.[24] They suggest that self-deception is properly understood as a particular kind of self-command, that is, "as making oneself *believe* something or *forget* something."[25] Canfield and Gustavson ask us to consider the following analysis of an "other-command":

1. Jones intends to make Smith do E.
2. Jones asks (commands, tells, etc.) Smith to do E.
3. Smith takes Jones' request (command, etc.) as a request to do E.
4. Smith complies with (obeys, etc.) Jones' request to do E.

If these same elements are applied to a reflexive command, we get a situation in which, for example:

1. Jones intends to make himself do E.
2. Jones tells himself to do E.
3. Jones takes his own request to do E.
4. Jones complies with his own request to do E.

Now Canfield and Gustavson admit that such a state of affairs is "odd sounding," but it is much less so when applied to a concrete example in which doing E involves overcoming certain obstacles. For instance, suppose that the task Jones faces is eating a food he detests or studying all night although he is very tired. In such cases it is not strange at all to speak of "self-commands." Using this model, Canfield and Gustavson maintain that a nonparadoxical analysis of self-deception is possible. By way of illustration, they consider a situation in which Jones is faced with evidence that overwhelmingly proves his son is guilty of some crime. In spite of this, Jones persists in his belief that his son is innocent. We would typically describe Jones here as deceiving himself. But we need not appeal to the awkward notion that Jones believes both that his son is guilty and not guilty (as the interpersonal model would have it). It is enough, they contend, to interpret self-deception here simply as belief in "belief-adverse circumstances," that is, belief "in the face of strong evidence to the contrary."[26] So conceived, the paradox of self-deception dissolves, since such cases need not be interpreted as involving simultaneous beliefs in contradictory propositions.

Is the Canfield-Gustavson proposal sound? It has the merit of eliminating the paradoxical element in self-deception, and it also squares with ordinary situations in which persons are described as deceiving themselves. But as Terence Penelhum notes, the prerequisites for self-deception offered by Canfield and Gustavson do not seem sufficient.[27] That is, there may be instances in which a person satisfies all the criteria in their account and yet is not genuinely self-deceived. Suppose Jones, in the case described above, believes in his son's innocence in the face of overwhelming evidence, but Jones does not fully appreciate how damning the evidence really is. His refusal to believe his son is guilty, then, might not suggest any self-deception whatsoever, yet such a case satisfies the conditions specified in Canfield and Gustavson's analysis. Thus, it seems, something must be added to complete their model.

Penelhum makes such an attempt with further criteria which, along with those already stipulated by Canfield and Gustavson, are thought to be individually necessary and jointly sufficient conditions for self-deception:

1. The subject must believe P in the face of strong evidence against P.
2. The subject must have knowledge of the evidence against P.
3. The subject must recognize the import of the evidence.[28]

These criteria, says Penelhum, "add up to a conflict-state in which there is partial satisfaction of the opposed criteria for belief and disbelief, with the subject's declarations likely to be against the evidence."[29]

Penelhum's additional criteria provide further clarity. But what does it mean to "recognize the import of the evidence?" Penelhum does not specify. It is natural to assume that such recognition involves understanding that not-P is implied by the evidence. But if this is so, then the subject must believe P as well as not-P, in which case we have returned to the original paradox. So the "self-command" strategy dead-ends with the same problem as the model of lying to oneself.

A different tack is taken by F. A. Siegler, who suggests that the term "self-deception" is, strictly speaking, a misnomer.[30] For there is no true deception involved in the phenomenon. Furthermore, expressions such as "I deceived myself" and "I knew all along," for all their suggestiveness, need not imply that a person actually once held two contradictory beliefs. According to Siegler, such remarks merely imply that the speaker believes she once persisted in a belief that she should have rejected (because of evidence to the contrary). Siegler elaborates: "Reflexive deception expressions function as warnings, accusations, attributions of unwarranted beliefs, as advice to reconsider what is considered to be mistaken, lamentations over the obtuseness or naivete of somebody, as spurs to resolve a new direction, etc. But none of these uses is a literal application of the ordinary model of 'Jones deceived Smith.'"[31]

Siegler certainly identifies an important function of "reflexive deception" expressions. We do often say such things as "I deceived myself" and "I knew all along" to declare that we once persisted in unwarranted or irrational belief. But the crucial question is whether this is the sole function of such expressions. Siegler does not even attempt to demonstrate this. Moreover, his account glosses over the real complexity of the phenomenon, for it does not deal with the whole matter of motive. No theory of self-deception is complete until it offers a reasonable account as to why persons stubbornly continue in unwarranted belief. Furthermore, the issue of whether persistent irrationality is intentional must be addressed.[32]

Moderate Strategies

In an effort to account for such dimensions of self-deception, various "moderate" accounts have been proposed. These aim to incorporate aspects of the partitioning and epistemic strategies without over-psychologizing the phenomenon or reducing it to simple irrationality.

Appeals to Motivated Bias

James Peterman defends what he conceives to be the traditional Cartesian approach to self-deception, construing it as "motivated avoidable error."[33] Peterman bases his interpretation of Descartes largely upon principles laid down in *Principles of Philosophy,* such as:

> That we deceive ourselves only when we form judgments insufficiently known to us.
> That whenever we err there is some fault in our method of action, or in the manner in which we use our freedom.
> Although we do not will to err, we yet err by our will.[34]

The will, according to Descartes, is absolutely free to affirm the truth of anything it wants, regardless of evidence. Now, the will can be, and often is, motivated by desires. Self-deception occurs when a person freely affirms a proposition that she desires to be true but which is not supported by the evidence, though she thinks it is. That is, self-deception occurs when one mistakenly, but avoidably, believes some falsehood that she desires to be true.

Peterman accepts this Cartesian account and spells it out as follows:

A person (A) is self-deceived in believing P if and only if

1. A believes that P.
2. It is false that P.
3. A might have recognized that P is false had he thought about P more carefully.
4. A part of the explanation for A's believing that P is that A desires that P.
5. A mistakenly believes that he believes that P because it is reasonable to do so.
6. A part of the explanation of A's belief that he believes P because it is reasonable to do so is his desire that P.[35]

According to this account, then, self-deception results from poor reasoning which in turn is attributable to a desire that corrupts the reasoning process. A similar approach to Peterman's has recently been offered by Alfred Mele, who argues that the key to understanding self-deception "is a proper appreciation of our capacity for acquiring and retaining motivationally biased beliefs."[36] Mele notes that there are a number of ways in which our desires can impact the way we treat data. He identifies four different psychological processes which motivate bias:

1. Negative misinterpretation—This occurs when one's desire that P causes her to underestimate (or completely discount) the significance of data counting against P. For example, the loyal mother's strong desire for her

son's goodness leads her to disregard trustworthy reports of her son's criminal activity as spurious.

2. Positive misinterpretation—This happens when one's desire for P causes him to interpret evidence against P as actually counting for it. The ladies' man demonstrates positive misinterpretation when he regards the desired woman's sneers as "playing hard to get."

3. Selective focusing—This occurs when one's desire that P leads her to attend to evidence supporting P to the exclusion of evidence against P. The loyal mother displays selective focusing when she concentrates on her son's academic achievements and good behavior earlier in his life rather than on recent police reports.

4. Selective evidence-gathering—This occurs when one's desire for P causes him to overlook obvious evidence against P and to locate less accessible evidence suggestive of P. The ladies' man is guilty of this when he ignores the woman's harsh refusals and takes her cordiality towards him as a sign of affection.[37]

Thus, according to Mele, the psychological dynamics of bias resulting from desire can be profound, though their effects are often entirely unintentional.[38]

The motivated bias approach seems to be an improvement on partitioning approaches and epistemic strategies, as it enjoys great explanatory power in paradigm cases of self-deception without the problems crippling the other two approaches. It does not presuppose an exotic psychological theory about mental compartments, subsystems, etc., nor does it attempt to reduce the phenomenon of self-deception to a simple instance of irrationality.

In spite of the plausibility of this strategy, it has been criticized for its failure to explain some classic instances of self-deception in which persons seem to have actual knowledge of something that they nevertheless deny. Newton da Costa and Steven French describe such a case that does not seem to fit within this model:

Consider the well-known example of a close friend or member of the family suddenly dying and the bereaved asserting,

"I know that x is dead but I just don't believe it." Such a person might not only assert this belief but might further reveal it through his or her behavior, such as continuing to lay a place for the dead person at the dinner table, for example. In such cases, it would seem that we are entitled to say that the relevant knowledge is typically present in the person's awareness, and is therefore conscious, the conflict with his or her belief leading to severe cognitive discomfort, which in turn is manifested in terms of bizarre forms of behavior.[39]

This scenario seems to identify a clear case of self-deception in which someone genuinely knows what one denies. Or worse, the person seems to believe and disbelieve the same proposition, thus suggesting, contrary to "motivated bias" theory, that self-deception is paradoxical after all, not merely a psychologically motivated mistake. What are we to make of this?

Mele himself deals with this problem by insisting that the person in this example could not be accurately described as believing that her loved one is dead, for regardless of one's verbal declarations "if a person *consistently* acts as one would act who believes that not-P, we have excellent reason to deny that he believes what he asserts."[40] That is, behavior is the ultimate indicator of belief. In the example, that the self-deceived person sets the table for the deceased conclusively suggests that she really does not believe the loved one is deceased, despite her words to the contrary.

Appeals to Subconscious Mental Processes

Some moderate strategies reject outright divisions of the mind but affirm sharp divisions of mental processing to explain self-deception. Such approaches preserve the notion that desire plays a key role in the phenomenon, but they return to the interpersonal model of self-deception and reintroduce some of the complex metapsychology of compartmentalist theories.

Mark Johnston's theory of "mental tropisms" is an excellent example of this approach. A mental tropism is a "purpose-serving mental mechanism" which is neither intentional nor entirely accidental.[41] It is a causal pattern of the mind's operations, including both rational and nonrational factors. Tropisms regularly influence decision-making and the formation of beliefs, their basic function being adaptive—for example, to relieve anxiety.

Steven Hales defends a version of Johnston's theory and offers the following analogy by way of explanation:

> We might think of the mind here as a tidal pool, with many different forces at work, and many different bits of flotsam within. At times some of the flotsam might clump together enough that a largish piece floats to the surface and becomes a full-fledged belief, or desire, or fear. And then it might break apart and fall from view. But it still remains within the pool. The fact that a piece of flotsam is not well-organized or formed enough to float to the top and engage in nice macro-level causal relations in no way means that it has no causal powers in the pool. The small bits of flotsam beneath the surface— barely noticeable emotions, little hunches, suspicions, attitudes that seem to vanish if you stare directly at them like faint stars— may well be causally involved in what is often called denial, repression, wishful thinking and the like. These are currents mostly below the surface of the water, which still may have visible effects above. Moreover, just as the activity of the tidal pool is complex but not random, so it is with the mind.[42]

In Hales's metaphor, tropisms are represented by subcurrents that sometimes affect the surface of the water. They are subconscious habits of the mind that impact a person's conscious thoughts and beliefs. Self-deception, according to this theory, occurs when a person persists in an unwarranted belief because of the influence of some tropism.

To apply this theory to a concrete case, consider the story of Dr. Androvna, an oncologist who is herself manifesting unmistakable symptoms of cancer. In spite of her expertise in cancer diagnosis, she ignores and misdescribes her symptoms. When friends ask about her condition, she avoids the issue altogether. On top of this, Dr. Androvna begins to engage in uncharacteristic behavior, organizing her financial affairs, drawing up a will, and contacting distant friends and relatives, bidding them farewell.[43] Dr. Androvna consciously believes she is healthy, an unwarranted belief to be sure. The theory of mental tropisms would suggest that this mistaken belief has been spawned by subintentional mental processes, including the fear of her impending death, regrets about untended friendships, sorrows about the relationships she will lose, and the grief her friends will experience upon her passing. The cumulative effect of these tropisms on Dr. Androvna's conscious thought is that she denies the import of evidence clearly pointing to her terminal condition.

A similar interpretation could be applied to cases discussed earlier, such as the loyal mother and the ladies' man. In fact, most paradigm cases of self-deception could be so plausibly explained. Still, the theory has a weakness. While the postulate of mental tropisms does not involve so elaborate a metapsychology as, say, Pears's doctrine of mental subsystems, it is still an exotic theory. How do we know mental tropisms even exist? And can a better description of them be provided beyond the vagaries and metaphors Johnston and Hales provide (e.g., habit, mechanism, subcurrent, flotsam, etc.)? A more complete elucidation and justification of the theory needs to be provided before it can be confidently embraced. In this regard the theory is incomplete.

THE EXISTENTIAL APPROACH

In a thorough treatment of self-deception, climaxing the philosophical furor over the subject in the 1960s, Herbert Fingarette developed a theory that turned the focus from belief to avowal. Self-deception, according to Fingarette, involves a refusal to "spell out" or explicitly acknowledge something about oneself: "The self-deceiver," he says, "is one who is in some way engaged in the world but who disavows the engagement, who will not acknowledge it even to himself as his. That is, self-deception turns upon the personal identity one accepts rather than the beliefs one has."[44]

Exactly what does it mean to "avow"? As Fingarette explains it, to make an avowal is to identify oneself in some way. It is to affirm, declare, or profess one's belonging to some particular tradition, family, culture, religion, country, or whatever.

For example, I am an avowed American and Protestant Christian. But just as one may avow belonging to some such category, one may "disavow" one's American heritage or Protestantism. This, of course, does not necessarily cause one to cease being either American or Protestant. Rather, it is a refusal to be identified as such.

Avowing need not include a verbal declaration. As Fingarette notes, "avowal is an inner act; which is to say that it is not in the ordinary sense an act at all."[45] It is more like a decision, "a purposeful self-expression." To explain this, Fingarette appeals to the notion of "spelling out." To spell out is to become "explicitly conscious," to say something "clearly and in a fully elaborated way, to make it perfectly apparent."[46] Thus, I may avow that I am an American by spelling out the fact that I was born in this country at a certain time and place. And I may avow my Protestantism by affirming my belief in salvation by grace through faith in Christ only and declaring my personal trust in him and his completed work to give me eternal life. By so doing I define an aspect of my personal identity as I explicitly acknowledge the nature of my faith commitment.

Disavowal, unlike avowal, does not involve any explicit statement about one's noncommitment. Rather, to disavow one need only refuse to avow, to refuse to explicitly acknowledge, a particular engagement. Such refusal to avow is manifested in a variety of ways, and Fingarette elaborates on three common forms.

Disavowal may be manifested by a person's simple incapacity to spell out her behavior, such as when the vegetarian is unable to acknowledge, much less explain, her sudden hamburger binge. Second, one may disavow an activity by isolating it from other activities that one does avow, such as the pornography addict who indulges his habit in secret. And third, one may disavow by denying responsibility for one's action. For instance, the woman in Sartre's example who flirts with a man toward whom she has no romantic feelings may simply deny that she is able to resist his subtle advances.

Thus, it is Fingarette's thesis that self-deception essentially involves a certain lack of moral integrity. But the question must be asked, What is the cause of self-deception in his view? Is it weakness of will? If so, Fingarette's model is too broad, as it would include instances of *akrasia*. That is, someone who is weak-willed or lacks self-control would then qualify as self-deceived on such an account. But this is surely mistaken, as *akrasia* and self-deception are distinct phenomena.

In defense of Fingarette's model, he could simply point out that to continue in a disavowed engagement is not to be weak-willed but to be a particular kind of person, to have a certain moral identity. As Fingarette notes, "the crux of the matter here is the *unacceptability* of the engagement to the person."[47] She continues in an activity with which she is incapable of identifying herself. She refuses to acknowledge the engagement as her own.

Fingarette's model of self-deception may be summarized as follows:

X is self-deceived if:

1. X has a continuing engagement (P) in the world.
2. X disavows P by refusing to spell out P, both to himself and to others.

The advance Fingarette's theory makes over moderate strategies is that it places an emphasis on the volitional aspect of self-deception neglected by other accounts. However, it is also weak where the other accounts are strong. That is, it seems to ignore the psychological and epistemic dimensions of the phenomenon emphasized by other models. Some commentators have argued that Fingarette's account focuses on the volitional manifestations of self-deception without offering a true analysis of self-deception itself.[48] In other words, Fingarette might be correct in suggesting that self-deceived persons disavow a particular engagement, but this is only to describe the symptom, not the disease itself. A complete account of self-deception must also explain the cognitive cause of the disavowal of the self-deceived.

A Hybrid Account

A full and adequate model of self-deception must account for both its cognitive and volitional dimensions. Thus, my own view of self-deception affirms aspects of two of the above models. Fingarette's existential account explains the volitional dimension of self-deception in terms of avowal, while the moderate strategy of Peterman and Mele appeals to motivated bias to explain the cognitive aspects of self-deception. These are compatible models because they address different dimensions of the phenomenon. Combining these two views, I believe, provides the appropriate balance, recognizing the relevance of both considerations. To date, in my opinion, this balance is best achieved by Robert Audi.

Audi defines self-deception as a dispositional, cognitive phenomenon, resulting from a person's unconscious knowledge of something that he consciously disavows, due to a strong desire that it not be true. Here is Audi's full account:

1. S unconsciously knows that not-P (or has reason to believe, and unconsciously and truly believes, that not-P);
2. S sincerely avows, or is disposed to avow sincerely, that P; and
3. S has at least one want which explains, in part, both why S's belief that not-P is unconscious and why S is disposed to avow that P, even when presented with what S sees is evidence against P.[49]

Like some moderate positions, this account recognizes the element of motivated bias (condition 3). Furthermore, Audi assumes a minimally "stratified" view of the self, appealing to "levels of consciousness."[50] And like Fingarette's existential approach, Audi incorporates the volitional element of avowal. It is somewhat softened, however, as he allows that a mere disposition to avow is required for self-deception (condition 2).

I believe Audi's position can be improved upon in two respects. First, his stratification of the self is unnecessary and may be eliminated without sacrificing any explanatory power in the model. Second, Audi's approach does not recognize that different cases of self-deception involve both motivated bias and the disposition to avow in varying degrees. It is here that I wish to modify Audi's general analysis.

I am convinced that self-deception has been such a confusing phenomenon for philosophers and psychologists because, first, it has both cognitive and volitional dimensions and, second, there are different kinds of self-deception, distinguished by the degree to which they are cognitive or volitional. Consider the case of the loyal mother. Her self-deception is caused by a strong desire for her son's innocence, which biases her thinking and results in a sincere but false belief in her son's innocence. She does not lack the ability to avow or "spell out" (as Fingarette would say) her belief in the goodness of her son. In fact, her biased thinking enables her to do so (e.g., "He is always so kind to me"; "He always has made good grades in school"; etc.). Rather, her self-deception is purely (or at least primarily) a case of motivated bias; her self-deception has a cognitive root.

Consider, on the other hand, Sartre's woman of "bad faith." Her self-deception is most emphatically volitional. She refuses to "admit to herself" her date's romantic interest and exhibits a sort of avoidance behavior that Fingarette's account captures so well—she refuses to avow her behavior as her own. The problem is not that she has a false belief but that she wills not to act according to a painfully true belief that she has.

These two paradigm cases exemplify the basic kinds of self-deception. They may be distinguished in terms of the critical point at which the self-deception occurs: prior to or after the act. The former I shall call "belief-formation phase" self-deception, and the latter, "reflection phase" self-deception. Instances of the former kind are defined by their cognitive nature, involving unintentional motivated bias, as Peterman and Mele suggest. Self-deception of the latter sort is volitional, as Fingarette would describe the phenomenon. The root of "belief-formation phase" self-deception, as the name suggests, is in the belief-forming process which is skewed by a strong desire for the truth of a false proposition. The causal root of "reflection phase" self-deception also pertains to desire, but following the act, where the person is concerned to preserve her act or "engagement" by ignoring certain details of her behavior or simply refusing to spell it out to herself. (See diagram on the following page.)

Whether self-deception is primarily "belief-formation phase" or "reflection phase" depends upon the degree of cognitive processing in the formation of one's belief. The more one is aware of the evidence for one's belief (whether bogus or not), the greater the ability and willingness to avow or spell out reasons for one's behavior. And the less one is aware of evidence for the belief upon which one's behavior is premised, the less the ability to avow it. Self-deceivers of the former sort are what we call rationalizers, while those in the latter case are ignorantly self-deceived.

The Two Kinds of Self-Deception

Belief-Formation Phase (Pre-act/Cognitive)		Reflection Phase (Post-act/Volitional)	
Evidence Against X		Pro-X Behavior	Disavowal of X (Refusal
	Unintentionally biased and false belief that X is true	(Act performed consistent with belief that X is true)	to spell out pro-X behavior)
Strong desire that X be true			

I am not suggesting that all cases of self-deception fall clearly into one or the other category. Combinations of "belief-formation phase" and "reflection phase" self-deception are possible and perhaps common. Take, for instance, the following reconstruction of the case of the "ladies' man." Because of a strong romantic attraction, he is motivated to embrace the false belief that the woman is interested in him. Still, her overwhelming refusals cause him serious doubts about her interest. In spite of this, he acts in ways that assume her interest, flirting with her and telling friends about his new flame. Here his disavowal, or refusal to spell out his behavior, completes the self-deception only partially begun at the cognitive stage. His self-deception is equal parts cognitive and volitional.

The obvious strength of this account is that it readily accommodates a variety of cases such as these, something the four models examined above are each too unidimensional to do. It seems the main problem plaguing the debate over self-deception has been theorists' stubborn insistence that each case be susceptible to precisely the same analysis.

WHEN HYPOCRISY INVOLVES SELF-DECEPTION

The final issue before us, lest we lose sight of our main quest, concerns the relationship between hypocrisy and self-deception. In our analysis of hypocrisy in chapter 2 it was noted that there are two kinds of hypocrites, amoralists and the self-deceived. So when is hypocrisy of the latter sort?

The answer to this question is that hypocrisy involves self-deception when it results from either (1) a false belief resulting from a motivated bias of some sort, (2) a disavowal of some continuing engagement in which one is involved, or (3) some combination of 1 and 2. Some examples will help to clarify.

Let's return to the cases discussed in the last chapter. Erin takes a strong animal rights position and is, therefore, a strict vegetarian. But her actions in eating a hamburger contradict this belief. If hers is a "belief-formation phase" self-deception, we may explain her behavior as resulting from a false belief (that eating meat in this situation is morally acceptable for her) resulting from a strong desire for meat. If her self-deception is "reflection phase," we would simply say that she is either unwilling or unable to avow this behavior, precisely because she does not believe that it is right. Or, of course, there may be a combination of these two elements explaining her self-deception and, ultimately, her hypocritical behavior.

The hypocrisy of Fran the politician can be analyzed in similar terms. Her strong desire for a victory in the election biases her belief about the moral justifiability of harsh language toward her staff. The will to win has an epistemic impact, persuading her that the means of spiteful behavior is justified by the end of victory at the polls. Or her false moral belief might take the form of a conviction that her staff "understands" that her words are not to be taken personally. Under either interpretation, it seems that hers is a "belief-formation phase" self-deception.

Finally, consider Chris, the lover of Scotch. He indulges excessively on a regular basis, in spite of the fact that he believes his behavior to be morally wrong. Unlike his brother's action, his is not due to weakness of will. Still, he disavows this behavior by refusing to spell it out to himself or to others. When confronted with the possibility of his being an alcoholic, he denies it emphatically and refuses to talk about it. Chris is a self-deceived hypocrite, and his self-deception is of the "reflection phase" type.

But what if neither Erin, Fran, nor Chris actually believe that, respectively, eating meat, harsh treatment of others, or alcohol abuse are morally wrong because there are no absolute moral values? In this case, they are not self-deceived. Rather, they lack moral seriousness. That is, they are amoralists, who are skeptical on all moral issues. Such persons are deceivers of others but not of themselves.

CONCLUSION

The subject of self-deception is complex and difficult, as is evidenced by the variety of theories proposed to explain it. One reason that self-deception defies easy description is that it involves both cognition and the will. Indeed, an adequate account of the phenomenon must duly attend to both of these aspects of human psychology. The view advocated here attempts to do just this.

Having analyzed self-deception, our basic definition of hypocrisy is now complete. But some major issues remain to be addressed. Specifically, hypocrisy must be assessed from the standpoints of moral philosophy and apologetics. And the phenomenon of moral weakness must be analyzed as well. These tasks will be taken up in the remaining chapters.

The Spirit Is Willing

Moral Weakness

An unknown compulsion bears me, all reluctant, down. Urged this way—that—on love's or reason's course, I see and praise the better: do the worse.

Ovid

It is but a shallow haste which concludeth insincerity from what outsiders call inconsistency.

George Eliot

We have found that there are two kinds of hypocrisy, one rooted in amoralism, the other in self-deception. The amoralist hypocrite acts inconsistently with principles that he only apparently believes in, for he lacks moral seriousness. The self-deceived hypocrite, on the other hand, acts inconsistently with his principles but denies it. His act is either justified by a motivated bias or else disavowed altogether. Either way, the self-deceived hypocrite admits no wrongdoing and has no regrets, as is the case with the amoralist hypocrite. But what of the person who does have regrets upon acting inconsistently with his own principles? (Clark, of the Scotch-drinking brothers discussed earlier, for example.) If his action is not hypocritical, how then are we properly to characterize it?

Typically, such cases are regarded as instances of moral weakness or *akrasia* (as termed by the ancient Greeks).[1] In this chapter we will explore this phenomenon and determine how (and if) *akrasia* is even possible. The pertinence of this issue to our study of hypocrisy should already be apparent, but it will be all the more so when we come to our analysis of the apologetic problem of hypocrisy in chapter 7.

The Philosophical Problem of *Akrasia* and Two Approaches to Solving It

We have all known persons who sincerely believe some action to be best and yet do the contrary. In fact, many would describe some of their own actions in this way. The phenomenon seems to be so common that it would hardly be regarded by most people as a philosophical "problem." But let us look more closely. Consider the following syllogism:

1. If someone judges that it would be better to do X than to do Y, then she wants to do X more than she wants to do Y.
2. If someone wants to do X more than she wants to do Y (and she is free to do either), then she will intentionally do X (if she does either).
3. Therefore, anyone who judges X to be better than Y will intentionally do X.[2]

This conclusion contradicts our "common" experience of persons acting intentionally against their best judgment. And the argument certainly seems valid. So what gives? This is the problem of *akrasia*.

How can this paradox be resolved? Historically, two basic approaches have been taken. One option is to surrender to the argument's logic and concede that all apparent cases of *akrasia* are illusory. This is the Socratic position. It denies the claim that a person can knowingly act against her better judgment, for to know the good, Socrates insisted, is to do it. The other option is to regard the above argument as flawed, questioning either the necessary connection between one's judgments and one's desires or between one's desires and one's intentional actions. The first and most important proponent of such an approach was Aristotle, who explained *akrasia* by appealing to the influence of nonrational aspects of the soul.

Contemporary accounts of *akrasia,* which have been numerous, fall roughly into these two categories. Philosophers either deny that genuine instances of the phenomenon actually exist, or else they defend some account as to how (and sometimes what) nonrational forces can determine actions, against the scruples of reason. In my own account I shall take the latter route. But let us first examine the traditional views.

THE SOCRATIC APPROACH

In Plato's dialogue *Protagoras,* Socrates defends the thesis that all immoral deeds arise ultimately from ignorance.[3] No one, he argues, willingly pursues what he knows to be evil. The gist of his reasoning is as follows. If we assume that persons always seek pleasure, then we know that no one would willingly choose pain over pleasure. And in deciding between two pleasurable courses of action, one will always choose the more pleasurable of the two. Furthermore, since people identify the good with what is pleasurable, it follows that all persons pursue what they conceive to be the greatest good. Therefore, as Socrates notes, "to make for what one believes to be evil, instead of making for the good, is not, it seems, in human nature."[4]

According to this view, *akrasia* is, strictly speaking, an illusion.[5] No one's better judgment is ever "mastered by pleasure." Rather, we sometimes make poor judgments when calculating which actions will have the most beneficial long-term results. We are prone, in particular, to prefer an immediate pleasure over a long-term pleasure and thus mistake the greatest good for an evil or a lesser good. But this is nothing more than to act on ignorance, to misconceive the good; it is not to willingly act against one's better judgment.

What are we to make of this argument Plato puts into the mouth of Socrates? As stated, it is most vulnerable in assuming psychological hedonism. While it is not entirely clear whether Socrates really believes this view or merely affirms it for the sake of argument against the "vulgar" folk who do, it is subject to serious criticism. First of all, there seem to be clear cases in which persons act for ends that produce great pain and diminish pleasure. For example, some "heroes" run great risks and even forsake their own lives to do what they believe to be right. Second, masochists or those who intentionally abuse themselves seem to seek pain, not pleasure.

Here an exponent of the Socratic view would appeal to a distinction made by Socrates in the *Protagoras,* namely that between perceived immediate goods and long-term goods. The hero who gives up his life for another is doing so for the long-term pleasure of those he helps. And masochists, paradoxically, actually take pleasure in their pain.

A further criticism regards the presumed identification of the pleasurable and the good. There are plenty of examples of actions that are pleasurable but not good, as well as good things that are not pleasurable. Drug abuse, illicit sex, and poor nutrition may all bring significant amounts of pleasure, but they are not morally good activities. And some instances of courage (e.g., a soldier in battle) and self-restraint (e.g., persevering in one's diet) can be quite painful.

Again, the defender of the Socratic view can explain these apparent counterexamples by appealing to the reasoning of the persons who engage in such activities. While it is plain to most that drug abuse over the long term results in great pain, it does not appear this way to the drug user. She sincerely believes otherwise and acts accordingly. So it is ignorance, not weakness of will, that constitutes her vice. Similarly, acts of great courage and self-restraint may be judged, correctly or not, to be routes to tremendous long-term pleasure, despite the risk or reality of intense short-term pain.

The Aristotelian Approach

Aristotle, who was the first to make a systematic analysis of *akrasia,* rejects the Socratic view (as he does on so many philosophical subjects), saying that it "plainly contradicts the observed facts."[6] Rather than acting in ignorance, Aristotle insisted, the *akrates* acts against her better judgment as a result of being overcome by passion.[7] The appetitive aspect of the soul, in such cases, gets the better of the rational part.

The key features of Aristotle's conception of moral weakness are best highlighted by contrasting it with the vice of intemperance or self-indulgence. To begin with, he makes it clear that *akrasia* is not properly understood as a vice, for "incontinence [*akrasia*] is contrary to choice while vice is in accordance with choice."[8] That is, the self-indulgent person chooses to act the way she does, based on the conviction that she acts rightly, though she is wrong. The *akrates,* on the other hand, is overcome by passion and acts against her better judgment. She knows the right thing to do but does the wrong thing anyway through no choice of her own. The Socratic view, Aristotle would say, makes just this confusion between moral weakness and the vice of self-indulgence. But it is the latter, not the former, that involves ignorance of the good.

It is because the self-indulgent person acts by choice that she is much less likely to repent than the *akrates.* As Aristotle explains, "Since the incontinent man is apt to pursue, not on conviction, bodily pleasures that are excessive and contrary to the right rule, while the self-indulgent man is convinced because he is the sort of man to pursue them, it is . . . the former that is easily persuaded to change his mind, while the latter is not."[9]

The *akrates* is apt to experience regret for allowing her passions to prompt her to violate the moral rule against her convictions. The self-indulgent person recognizes no such violation and thus is "like a city that uses its laws, but has wicked laws to use."[10]

Aristotle distinguishes the incontinent person from the continent [*egkrates*] person on the basis of whether his mind controls his behavior: "the incontinent man, knowing that what he does is bad, does it as a result of passion, while the continent man, knowing that his appetites are bad, refuses on account of his rational principle to follow them."[11] Unlike the *akrates,* the continent person successfully exercises moral dominion over himself by following reason. In this respect, the most vicious persons may be continent, for at least they are ruled by their moral convictions, however faulty they might be.

The Aristotelian account of moral weakness has received at least as much criticism as the alternative Socratic account. One objection addresses Aristotle's assumption that the *akrates* "knows better" than his actions indicate. This seems to beg the question, for it presupposes genuine knowledge of what is best, the very point rejected by the Socratist. But if a person acts in direct contradiction to her belief, then one might doubt for just this reason that she truly has that belief. Such criticism may appeal to Gilbert Ryle's distinction between "dispositions" and "occurrences."[12] A disposition is a tendency or proneness to behave in a certain way, while occurrences are unique or episodic.[13] By Ryle's account, the concepts "belief" and "knowledge" are dispositional, not occurrent, as Aristotle seems to assume. Thus, a person's behavior is sufficient grounds for concluding what she really believes about the rightness or wrongness of an action, regardless of what she might say or think she believes.

In reply to this criticism, one may reject Ryle's account of belief and knowledge as counterintuitive. Ordinary experience shows that some beliefs are indeed episodic or brief in duration. And we have all had the experience of acting in a way that does not "match up" with a belief that we have sincerely held for a long period of time. These, presumably, are some of the "observed facts" to which Aristotle refers as contradicting the Socratic view.

A second objection, pertaining to the matter of will, is more serious. How can a person act against his choice, as Aristotle suggests? If a person does not genuinely choose his action, then in what sense can the action be meaningfully said to be his? Wouldn't this instead be a case of compulsion? And if so, then it seems the *akrates* could never be responsible or blameworthy for his incontinent actions. Here the Aristotelian is likely to appeal to the fact that while the *akrates'* choice does not cause his action, his passions do. So the action remains that of the *akrates,* though its cause is emotion or some other psychic phenomenon rather than rational deliberation.

The most common objection to the Aristotelian account by contemporary scholars regards its questionable assumptions about the nature of the soul. In the previous chapter we saw how problematic compartmentalist theories of mind can be. Aristotle's doctrine, which divides the soul into rational and nonrational parts, is subject to similar criticisms. Specifically, are we to understand these aspects of the soul as differing functions of a singular entity or as distinct subentities? If the former, then the *akrates'* soul functions in a self-contradicting way when performing an incontinent act, which is incoherent. If the latter, then further problems arise, especially regarding personal identity. For instance, is a person just one of these subentities of the soul, such as the rational part? If so, then to be overcome by passion seems more like compulsion than moral weakness. And to hold that a person is a collective of these parts of the soul is to deny the unity of the self, which seems to be at least as much of an "observed fact" as the occurrence of *akrasia.*

CONTEMPORARY ACCOUNTS OF *AKRASIA*

Recent discussions of the phenomenon of moral weakness have focused on many of the same problems addressed by the ancient Greek philosophers. Although writers on the subject usually fall clearly into one or the other of the two traditional positions, some do propose hybrid accounts.

Hare's Hybrid Account

The British moral philosopher R. M. Hare attempts such a hybrid account.[14] Hare defends an ethical theory called "moral prescriptivism." This is the view that moral beliefs and judgments are prescriptive and embody imperatives. To have a moral conviction, then, is to affirm a rule that is binding on all persons in similar circumstances. And to believe "X is good" is to command oneself "Let me do X." So how are we to explain situations when a person believes an action to be good but fails to do it? Ruling out hypocrisy as a genuine candidate for *akrasia,* Hare suggests that "two interpretations of this phenomenon become possible. . . . The first is that the person who accepts some moral judgment but does not act on it is actually giving commands to himself but is unable to obey them because of a recalcitrant lower nature or 'flesh'; the other is that he is, in his whole personality or real self, ceasing to prescribe to himself. . . ."[15]

The first explanation here appeals to psychological compulsion, where a person simply cannot act as he thinks he ought. The second regards persons who "lack complete moral conviction," those who use the word "ought" but who are nevertheless "not so *sure* that they ought, as to commit themselves to action."[16]

At first blush, Hare seems to incorporate elements of both classical points of view on *akrasia.* In the first case, he admits that the will may succumb to nonrational forces of the mind, which is reminiscent of Aristotle's view. In the second case, he suggests the Socratic position that *akrasia* is sometimes due to a lack of knowledge of the good.

However, in neither of these cases do we have genuine *akrasia* as commonly understood. In the former case, Hare reduces moral weakness to psychological compulsion, but this is counterintuitive. Weakness is not powerlessness.[17] Furthermore, to be utterly unable to carry out an action removes moral culpability. But the morally weak person *is* morally culpable for her action (or failure to act).

The possibility proposed by Hare of conceiving of *akrasia* as resulting from a lack of moral conviction also flies in the face of the usual understanding of moral weakness as involving sincere moral belief combined with a failure to act according to that conviction. This is the paradox that any adequate account of *akrasia* must solve. But there is no paradox in the case of a person doing X when she suspects the act is morally wrong but is not fully convinced.

But what if Hare really means to suggest that in these latter cases *akrasia* is just an illusion? Perhaps his point is that if a person's action is not compelled by psychological forces, then there must be lack of moral conviction. If this is what he intends to say, then his view ignores what seem to be the facts of common experience, as some people seem to act in defiance of their full moral conviction. Because of this problem, Hare should offer positive empirical evidence or examples to support his theory. But as one critic has noted, he does not do this, and as a result his theory is irrefutable.[18] Of course, since he presumably aims to account for certain data of human experience, this is a philosophical demerit, not an asset.

Davidson's Socratic Proposal

Donald Davidson proposes a view that is Socratic in the sense that it regards *akrasia* as a kind of irrationality.[19] The key to solving the riddle of incontinence, Davidson says, lies in recognizing a distinction between two kinds of practical reasoning: conditional and unconditional. Unconditional practical reasoning evaluates actions *prima facie* or "on the face of things," whereas practical reasoning that is conditional evaluates actions all things considered.[20] He suggests that it is one's rational duty to act intentionally on the basis of conditional evaluations. That is, one should "perform the action judged best on the basis of all available relevant reasons," which Davidson calls the "principle of continence."[21] It is precisely in his failure to abide by this rational principle that the *akrates* goes wrong. He acts on his *prima facie* judgment rather than his judgment "all things considered." So the *akrates'* action is irrational. This is why "the attempt to read reason into [his] behavior is necessarily subject to frustration."[22] And the incontinent person recognizes "in his own intentional behavior something essentially surd."[23]

Davidson's account is an inventive version of the Socratic view, but there are problems with his position. For instance, his distinction between unconditional and conditional practical reasoning is questionable when applied to real life decision-making. Granted, the distinction can be made in the abstract. But in practical affairs, aren't all our moral judgments arrived at "all things considered," at least in the sense that they are relative to all we know? And when a person gathers new information implying the propriety of a different course of action, either his conviction changes accordingly or it does not. If it changes, he is continent. If it does not, he is more likely self-deceived.

Furthermore, even granting that Davidson's distinction applies to real-life situations, he is far from showing that it is impossible that one could act contrarily to one's *prima facie* judgment.[24] Also, Davidson must explain why the *akrates* ignores his judgment "all things considered" in favor of his *prima facie* judgment. There must be some causal explanation as to why the lesser consideration (in terms of rational evidence) overcomes the better, more informed judgment. It is precisely here that Aristotle would insist that passion overcomes the *akrates'* rational convictions.

Watson's Aristotelian Approach

In the Aristotelian tradition, Gary Watson sees virtue as a sort of trained skill or ability. He regards *akrasia* as a vice or lack of self-control. Morally weak persons do not necessarily lack the proper values or knowledge. Nor are they necessarily subject to stronger desires than morally strong persons. "What makes the former weak," Watson says, "is that they give in to desires which the possession of the normal degree of self-control would enable them to resist."[25] The incontinent person, then, *does not* resist wrongful desire because she *cannot*. But this is not to say that her action is compelled, for "an agent is motivated by a compulsive desire if *no* degree of training and discipline would have enabled him or her to resist."[26] The *akrates,* then, is subnormal in terms of moral strength. And her fault actually consists in her failure in the development or maintenance of the relevant capacities for overcoming wrongful desire. For it is this negligence that precipitates her wrongdoing.

Watson's account is a definite improvement upon those of Hare and Davidson. For one thing, it makes sense of the common experience of "giving in" to temptation and indulging in behaviors we sincerely believe to be wrong, all things considered. Moreover, we do ordinarily regard the *akrates* as lacking self-control, at least on the occasion of yielding to temptation. This theory does not, however, account for those cases where even the normally self-controlled person succumbs to temptation. How are we to explain the occasional lapses of the otherwise continent? And a further question needs to be answered: What is it in a person that one fails to control when she is weak-willed? In other words, what aspect of the "self" overcomes one's better judgment in an incontinent act? Watson's account of *akrasia* is a good one, as far is it goes, but it does not go far enough. For we are seeking a complete causal explanation for such behaviors which can provide answers to these sorts of questions.

King-Farlow's Compartmentalist Account

Some philosophers have appealed to a division of the self to provide such an explanation, much as we saw in the previous chapter's discussion of "compartmentalist" theories of self-deception. The account of John King-Farlow provides an excellent example of this. King-Farlow explains moral weakness by appealing to the notion of a "master-self," which he describes as "the normal intrapersonal arbiter among the warring factions that help to constitute . . . an agent's mind."[27] It is that "subpersona" of the self, among the many composing it, which typically decides the course of action to take. *Akrasia* occurs when the master-self, in spite of its desires for perceived goods, is overcome by certain contradictory desires of "rival agents" within the self.

Now King-Farlow is fully aware of the skepticism that compartmentalist accounts such as his often meet. However, he explains that "where the objects and signs of conflicting *intentions* (conscious, unconscious or mixed intentions), attain a certain richness and complexity which attest to a *divided person's* wanting those objects, the introduction of talk about *Personae* is more likely to be a step towards realism rather than just an exercise in psychic cartooning."[28]

King-Farlow's theory claims to have identified the aspects of the self that overwhelm one's better judgment and give rise to incontinence. This is a move in the right direction, but in one respect it is a move too far. In the last chapter we noted some of the difficulties with similar accounts of self-deception, not the least of which is their lack of coherence. King-Farlow's theory fares no better. To the extent that his theory explains *akrasia,* he sacrifices the unity of the self. Who or what is my "self"? If it is the master-self, then how can I be held responsible for the actions of my other sub-selves when I act incontinently? But if the subpersonae of my mind are also my selves, then *I* have no unity (i.e., I am not one, but many).

Additionally, King-Farlow's justification for positing the existence of subpersons (appealing to "a richness and complexity" of talk about conflicting intentions) is inadequate. He has hardly provided the "good and sufficient reasons" required by Ockham's razor for multiplying entities (in this case, the subentities of the mind). I am as skeptical as most critics on this matter. Granted, intrapersonal conflict is aptly described using the metaphor of subpersonae, but why treat these metaphors as metaphysical realities? No doubt King-Farlow would respond by insisting that short of doing so, no adequate account of moral weakness can be provided. But this remains to be seen.

The Pears-Stocker Account

What is needed is an explanation of how a person can lose self-control that does not sacrifice the unity of the self. One promising account is offered by Michael Stocker. He claims "that (believed) goods, at least some obvious and important (believed) goods, can 'fail' to attract us, at least at times."[29] Or to put it more generally, "something can be good and one can believe it to be good without being in a mood or having an interest or energy structure which inclines one to seek or even desire it."[30] Also, we can be positively attracted to what we believe to be bad, and these desires can and sometimes do move us to action against our better judgment. Our reason for so acting, Stocker says, is various "maladies of spirit" such as despair, tiredness, and feelings of futility and appetites that override our sincere beliefs about the good. He rejects the Socratic notion that "to know the good is to do it" as a psychologically naive view that ignores the subversive power of noncognitive elements that move the will. One's mood, energy, interests, and so forth constitute what Stocker calls a "mediating structure" through which one's beliefs are filtered and affected. Such psychological dynamics can serve to disconnect motivation from evaluation, resulting in behavior that goes against one's better judgment.

A similar explanation is provided by David Pears. He argues that there is not a necessary connection between one's judging an action best and one's doing it. What he calls "brazen *akrasia*" results from a "momentarily motivated lack of integration" of deliberate valuation in the prompting of action.[31] In other words, physical appetites, for example, may lead the incontinent person to disregard rational evaluation of the action she is tempted to perform. While she judges the action to be wrong, this conviction is ignored in the instant that she wills her action. As Pears notes, "a physical appetite concentrates its maximal force in the moment immediately before the action."[32] While some would protest that the *akrates'* behavior itself shows that deliberation led her to perform her action, Pears maintains that this Socratic objection "exaggerates the degree of integration maintained by normal human agents and consequently uses an excessively simple behavioral criterion of judging best."[33]

The Pears-Stocker account succeeds where Watson's theory says too little and King-Farlow, in one sense, says too much. Pears and Stocker identify the root of the loss of self-control in certain noncognitive psychological dynamics of the mind. In this way, they take seriously our common sense intuitions about conflicting desires and intentions. But they resist the temptation to compartmentalize the mind and spoil the unity of the self.[34] A further merit of this account is that it recognizes that nonrational forces affect one's will, without implying that *akrasia* is a kind of compulsion.

I favor such a view as that offered by Pears and Stocker combined with the virtue-theory approach of Watson (*a la*

Aristotle). I think the former must be supplemented by the latter because an explanation is needed as to why some people are much less inclined to be overcome by their physical appetites or "maladies of spirit" than others. We are all familiar with persons who seem to have a greater trained ability of self-control than others. Or perhaps more convincingly, some persons are able to "grow" in self-control and improve the skill of resisting the demands of the "lower nature" (as Hare would put it).

BIBLICAL REFLECTIONS ON AKRASIA

The account of *akrasia* just outlined fits especially well with the biblical data on the subject. As we shall see, the Scriptures (1) imply the reality of *akrasia,* or situations in which one acts against her better judgment, (2) explain such moral failure by appealing to the "lower" (sin) nature in human beings, and (3) recommend the development of self-control in order to master its urges. In the remainder of this chapter I shall address the first two of these biblical themes. The matter of self-control will be discussed in the next chapter.

The Scriptures are at odds with the Socratic view in acknowledging the reality of *akrasia*. This is seen both in the narrative and explicit teaching of Scripture. The most vivid illustration of moral weakness is Peter's denial of Christ in Matthew 26. The salient points of this narrative, for our purposes, are as follows.

First, it appears that Peter genuinely believed it best not to deny Jesus. This is suggested not only by his vigorous insistence that he would not deny Jesus but also by his passionate response to his failure to keep his word. Second, he denied Jesus anyway. There is no mistaking this, since he did so not once, but thrice. And third, Peter deeply regretted what he had done, as is indicated by his weeping afterwards.

It would appear that here we have a clear biblical instance of *akrasia*. How might the account of *akrasia* previously sketched explain Peter's behavior? More specifically, what noncognitive psychological dynamics could have been operant upon his will to move him to deny Jesus? The circumstances of Peter's denial strongly suggest that fear motivated him to act as he did. It is reasonable to suppose that Peter sensed he would be in real danger if he was identified with Jesus. While in his more lucid moments (e.g., earlier that night in the presence of Jesus and like-minded disciples) Peter's rational deliberations led him to the clear conviction that the best thing in such a situation would be to die with Jesus, under pressure he buckled. His rational convictions were probably overrun by just the sorts of "maladies of spirit" identified by Stocker: despair (because of the arrest of his Lord), tiredness (due to emotional trauma and lack of sleep), and feelings of futility (there was nothing Peter could do to fix the situation).

If the case of Peter's denial is not persuasive scriptural evidence for the reality of *akrasia,* the explicit New Testament teaching is. Consider the words of Jesus to his disciples as he despairs over their failure to pray with him in his final hours: "the spirit is willing," he says, "but the body is weak."[35] Here Jesus alludes to the opposition between what one desires and what one actually does, essential to cases of *akrasia.*

But the most pregnant passages regarding moral weakness pertain to the "sinful nature" of human beings. One of these is Galatians 5:16–17, where Paul writes, "Live by the Spirit, and you will not gratify the desires of the sinful nature. For the sinful nature desires what is contrary to the Spirit, and the Spirit what is contrary to the sinful nature. They are in conflict with each other, so that *you do not do what you want*" (emphasis added).

Not only does this passage contradict the Socratic account, it makes plain just where this view goes wrong. If we recall from the beginning of this chapter the syllogism that constituted the "problem" of *akrasia,* the second premise stated that if someone wants to do X more than she wants to do Y, then she will intentionally do X. This premise is flatly contradicted by Paul's statement in Galatians 5:17. Thus, we have biblical evidence that the Socratic view is false and that the argument used to support it is unsound.

Romans 7:14–25, another Pauline treatment of the subject, expresses the same idea, but this time from a first-person perspective:

[14]We know that the law is spiritual; but I am unspiritual, sold as a slave to sin. [15]I do not understand what I do. For what I want to do I do not do, but what I hate I do. [16]And if I do what I do not want to do, I agree that the law is good. [17]As it is, it is no longer I myself who do it, but it is sin living in me. [18]I know that nothing good lives in me, that is, in my sinful nature. For I have the desire to do what is good, but I cannot carry it out. [19]For what I do is not the good I want to do; no, the evil I do not want to do—this I keep on doing. [20]Now if I do what I do not want to do, it is no longer I who do it, but it is sin living in me that does it.

[21]So I find this law at work: When I want to do good, evil is right there with me. [22]For in my inner being I delight in God's law; [23]but I see another law at work in the members of my body, waging war against the law of my mind and making me a prisoner of the law of sin at work within my members. [24]What a wretched man I am! Who will rescue me from this body of death? [25]Thanks be to God—through Jesus Christ our Lord!

This passage clearly affirms the reality of *akrasia*. First, Paul asserts that he knows the good and desires it (vv. 16, 18, 19, 21). Second, he does not do the good he desires but rather does the evil he does not desire (vv. 15, 19). It follows that what one sincerely wants is not necessarily what one does. That is to say, the Socratic thesis is mistaken (and the second premise of the syllogism above is again refuted).

It is also evident from this passage—assuming that Paul speaks not just for himself—that there is an immoral tendency present within a person that is in conflict with his knowledge of the good. This element, as in the Galatians 5 passage, he refers to as the "sinful nature" (v. 18) but also as "sin" (vv. 17, 20), "evil" (v. 21), and "law of sin" (v. 23). Also, it is clear by Paul's account that the sin within us has the capacity to overwhelm our knowledge of the good in terms of prevailing influence on the will. Although the mind both knows the good and deeply desires it, the sinful nature exercises a leverage on the will powerful enough to direct it contrarily. And so it seems that even Christians should be expected to experience difficulty and occasional defeat in their struggle with sin.

It may be asked, however, who is really speaking in this passage? Is it the Christian, such as Paul himself, or the spiritually unregenerate person? If it is the latter, then arguably the person in question does not really "know" the good that he fails to do and the Socratic view is not rebutted by this passage. If the former, then the speaker does indeed know the good but acts contrarily, which confirms the Aristotelian thesis. Just whose testimony is this?

This question has generated much debate among biblical scholars. Some, such as Douglas Moo, have maintained that the experience described in this passage is that of the non-Christian. Specifically, says Moo, "Paul is looking back, from his Christian understanding, to the situation of himself, and other Jews like him, living under the law of Moses."[36] The reason for drawing this conclusion is that the passage seems to suggest that the speaker is regularly defeated by his sin. On the other hand, even to recognize one's own sinfulness, as does the person described in Romans 7, is evidence that one is in fact spiritually regenerate. As Martin Luther observes, "no one will declare himself wretched except one who is a spiritual man."[37] Similarly, Martin Lloyd-Jones argues, "the unregenerate man never condemns sin in the way this man does who says, 'What I do, I do not allow; I do not approve of it.' The unregenerate man never uses such language. Neither does he ever say that he hates sin."[38] Whether or not this argument is judged to be compelling hinges upon one's view of the unregenerate human nature. Calvinists usually adopt the "postconversion" interpretation of this passage because they see humans in their natural state as totally morally depraved. Arminians, on the other hand, are more likely to take the "preconversion" view, largely because they do not view the natural moral condition of human beings to be so grave.[39]

For my own part, I find the postconversion interpretation of Romans 7 to be the more compelling, and this for several reasons. First, Paul uses the first-person voice and does so exclusively throughout verses 14–25, which certainly provides *prima facie* evidence that Paul is speaking for himself. But more than this, he abruptly switches from the past tense, which he uses in discussing his condemnation under the law from verses 8–13, to the present tense at verse 14, suggesting that the ensuing description of his struggle with sin is to be contrasted with his former unregenerate state.[40]

Second, I believe the Calvinist moral anthropology to be biblical, and given that human beings are so depraved, the preconversion interpretation cannot account for (1) the condemnation of sin (vv. 15, 18, and 24), (2) the desire to do the good (vv. 15, 18, 19, and 21), or (3) the confession of "delight in God's law" (v. 22). Granting the doctrine of original sin, it is difficult to see how even from the perspective of Arminian theology one could attribute such positive moral and spiritual capacities to the unregenerate person.

Third, the postconversion interpretation is congruent with the experience of many Christians. I am not suggesting that the regenerate person normally experiences exasperation and defeat in her battle with sin. I am saying that many Christians do experience seasons of such exasperation, specifically when not relying on the moral empowerment of the Holy Spirit for moral strength.[41] Even when blessed with success in obedience to the moral law, the Christian life is marked by continuous struggle. Isn't this the whole point of repeated biblical exhortations to Christians' persevering in their "struggle against sin"[42] and the "sinful desires, which war against your soul"?[43]

The conclusion that the Bible acknowledges *akrasia* does not hinge on any particular interpretation of Romans 7:14–25. The postconversion interpretation of this passage does, however, provide for a much stronger defense of this view. In any case, the biblical data conclusively refutes the Socratic approach to *akrasia*. Moral weakness is a real and troublesome fact of human experience, for the Christian no less than the unbeliever.

CONCLUSION

The philosophical problem of moral weakness or *akrasia* is difficult and confusing. How can a person act inconsistently with what she sincerely believes to be the best course of action? There are two principal perspectives on this issue. The Socratic approach regards the phenomenon as essentially illusory, maintaining that persons only appear to act against their better judgment. *Akrates* really don't know the good they are supposed to do. But this view is counterintuitive and fails to account for some plain facts of human experience. The Aristotelian approach, however, has difficulties of its own, particularly regarding assumptions about the nature of the soul. Contemporary versions of each of these views face similar difficulties, but all things considered, some version of the Aristotelian view seems best. I endorse the view that *akrasia* involves acting against one's better judgment due to the influence of certain noncognitive forces of the mind. This position not only is philosophically defensible but also fits comfortably with the biblical data.

The Now
and the Not Yet

Sin, Self-Control, and Sanctification

Every saint has a past and every sinner a future.

Oscar Wilde

It is part of the cure to want to be cured.

Seneca

The previous chapter concluded that persons act against their better judgment when their rational deliberations are overcome by certain noncognitive forces of the mind. In this respect, the *akrates* is guilty of a loss of self-control. This view of *akrasia* aligns with the key biblical texts pertaining to the subject. This chapter will continue this discussion by (1) exploring the theological concept of original sin and its relation to *akrasia,* (2) identifying some further causes of *akrasia,* (3) discussing the virtue of self-control and how the *akrates* may be reformed, and (4) discussing the theological concept of sanctification.

ORIGINAL SIN: THE NATURAL TENDENCY TOWARD *AKRASIA*

An essential tenet of Christian anthropology is that human beings are fundamentally morally flawed. God has given us his moral law and commanded us to obey, but none have succeeded in doing so perfectly. As Paul says, "All have sinned and fall short of the glory of God."[1] Likewise, the prophet Isaiah declares, "We all, like sheep, have gone astray, each of us has turned to his own way."[2] And the psalmist remarks sadly, "There is no one who does good, not even one."[3] But the biblical view is not just that we fail to live up to the moral standard; we do so by nature.

The Scriptures speak frequently to this seemingly innate tendency toward moral failure, a notion epitomized in King David's despairing words, "Surely I was sinful at birth, sinful from the time my mother conceived me."[4] Since the early church fathers, Christian theologians have spoken with one voice about the severity of our sin problem. Augustine was one of the first to refer to it as "original sin," its root being the sin of Adam. "That one sin," says Augustine, "admitted into a place where such perfect happiness reigned, was of so heinous a character, that in one man the whole human race was originally, and as one may say, radically condemned."[5] As our representative head, Adam's singular moral rebellion and subsequent condemnation became our own.

Aquinas contrasts original sin to the "original justice" intrinsic to human nature before the fall. Prior to sin's entrance into the world, humans were naturally disposed toward obedience to the moral law. But now we are naturally disposed toward evil. Aquinas uses the analogy of physical illness in describing original sin as "an inordinate disposition, arising from the destruction of the harmony which was essential to original justice, even as bodily sickness is an inordinate disposition of the body, by reason of the destruction of that equilibrium which is essential to health."[6]

The Reformers were especially emphatic about the power of the sinful impulse in the human heart. Martin Luther writes that "Satan and man, being fallen and abandoned by God, cannot will good, i.e., things which please God or which God wills, but are ever turned in the direction of their own desires, so that they cannot but seek out their own."[7] Because of this, according to Luther, any moral goodness manifest in human deeds or words could only come through the direct work of the Holy Spirit.

Heartily affirming Luther's diagnosis, John Calvin called original sin "a hereditary depravity and corruption of our nature, diffused into all parts of the soul."[8] It is a perversity into which we are born, so that "even infants themselves, while they carry their condemnation along with them from the mother's womb, are guilty not of another's fault but their own."[9] This innate perversity is a complete depravity, in Calvin's view, not a mere loss of our original righteousness. "The whole man is overwhelmed—as by a deluge—from head to foot, so that no part is immune from sin and all that proceeds from him is to be imputed to sin."[10]

Similarly, Jonathan Edwards referred to original sin as an "evil tendency or propensity," but he went on to define "tendency" in this context as a "prevailing liableness or exposedness" which serves as "a foundation for the constancy, or strongly prevailing probability" of a particular event.[11] Edwards also pointed out that given the preponderance of actual sin among human beings, we can infer the sinful depravity of the human heart as the cause, because "a steady effect argues a steady cause."[12] Thus, the reality of original sin is empirically verifiable.

Among Protestant theologians it is not only Calvinists who have so emphasized the seriousness of the human sin problem. John Wesley eloquently expounds upon it, offering just the sort of empirical verification (via introspection) of original sin implied by Edwards:

> If you . . . would but look into yourself daily, and observe all the sinful and irregular turns of your own heart; how propense you are to folly, in greater or less instances; how soon appetite and passion oppose reason and conscience; how frequently you fall short of the demand of the perfect law of God; how thoughtless and forgetful you are of your Creator; how cold and languishing your affection to Him; how little delight you have in virtue, or in communion with God:

> Could you think you are such an innocent and holy creature
> as God at first created you? . . . Surely a more accurate obser-
> vation of your own heart must convince you, that you your-
> self are degenerated from the first rectitude of your nature.[13]

Such is the witness of some of the great Christian theologians on the reality and severity of sin. Note that they make
no suggestion of original sin being an entity or faculty distinct
from the human mind. Rather, it refers to nothing else but the
corrupt moral condition of our nature. To say that human
beings have a "sinful nature" (as does Paul in Galatians 5 and
Romans 7) is not the same as saying that we have a "sin nature"
that is distinct from our human nature. The biblical view is
not that we have two natures but that our human nature is
morally tainted or sinful, hence the "sinful nature" of which
Paul speaks.

FREEDOM, COMPULSION, AND THE TENDENCY TO SIN

Given this doctrine of sin, and the concomitant position
that *akrasia* involves giving in to the demands of one's sinful nature although one knows better, does it follow that incontinence occurs by compulsion? The answer depends upon
what one means by compulsion. If the term is not intended
so as to deny human freedom and moral responsibility, there
is no reason to reject this implication. However, if compulsion is understood to be inconsistent with freedom and responsibility (as is usually the case), then, from a biblical standpoint, compulsion cannot be implied by this tendency to sin.
For the Scriptures (as well as common sense) clearly affirm
human freedom and moral responsibility.

But now let us look again at Paul's statement in Romans
7:20 that "if I do what I do not want to do, it is no longer I
who do it, but it is sin living in me that does it." This remark
does *prima facie* suggest that he is under the influence of
something irresistible. Can Paul be taken to mean here that
he is not responsible for his sin? On the contrary, such an
interpretation ignores a central theme of Romans (not to men-
tion Paul's other epistles)—that human beings deserve God's

wrath. His is not a "devil made me do it" theology of sin. What, then, are we to make of this remark?

I see two possible lines of response, each of which makes sense of Paul's assertion in verse 20 and respects our intuitions as well as the biblical testimony about human freedom and moral responsibility. First, Paul's remark might simply refer to the fact that were his nature not fallen, he would not sin. To have a sinful nature is to be tainted by something alien to one's essence as a human being. So to say that "it is no longer I who [sins], but it is sin living in me" is just to underscore this fact. And yet he is no less responsible, for it is his nature that is corrupt, and it is he who chooses to act sinfully. In so many words, this is to say that when Paul says "it is no longer I who do it," he is speaking hyperbolically, not literally.

A second explanation relies on the interpretation of Romans 7 as referring to the experience of the Christian, as opposed to that of the unregenerate person. We may regard the sinful nature as a powerful contributing cause to determine one's choice, but it is not irresistible. It is well within the Christian's power, by the help of the Holy Spirit, to resist the impulses of this "lower" aspect of his nature. And to the extent that the Christian fails, he succumbs to something that is no longer morally definitive for him. For he has been given a new desire for the good and a new ability, though not a compulsion, to carry it out. Or, using Edwards' expression, for the Christian there is no longer "a prevailing probability" that he will sin, though there certainly remains a strong inclination in that direction on various occasions, perhaps just the sorts of occasions to which Paul refers.

But now it may be asked, if sin is not compulsory, then how can we be sure that all will sin or have sinned? In response to this question, it is useful to distinguish two aspects of original sin, namely, pollution and guilt. The pollution of sin pertains to the sinful depravity of a person's character that is the inheritance of all descendants of Adam. This accounts for the propensity to sin. The guilt of sin regards our liability to punishment, also inherited from Adam but in a different sense. The guilt of original sin is imputed to us through the sin of our representative head, Adam. As Paul notes, "the result of one trespass was condemnation for all men."[14] So even prior to a person's actual violation of the law of God in deed, word, or thought, he is both guilty of and polluted by sin. Now the proper response to the question, whether there is any guarantee that, in fact, all are sinners, should be self-evident. All are born with a sinful nature (pollution) and are guilty before God (through imputation of Adam's sin).

However, most Christians believe that during any person's lifetime she is guaranteed to actually sin at some time or another (if not many times daily). The question now becomes, What of the possibility of a person successfully resisting temptations her entire life and avoiding lapses into the actual performance of sin? Is this possible or is even this lapse into sin guaranteed? And if it is guaranteed that all will sin (assuming they live into adulthood), then mustn't it also be the case that for any person, on some particular occasion she will sin by compulsion, that is, by causal necessity? For how else could her eventual actual sinning be guaranteed rather than, say, highly probable?

This line of argument attempts to show that commitment to the idea of guaranteed performance of sin at some time or another during a lifetime commits one to belief in compulsory sin at a particular time. To present the argument more explicitly, consider these two propositions (where "normal lifetime" denotes one's living into adulthood):

(P1) For any given person, it is guaranteed that *at one time or another* during a normal lifetime she will sin.

(P2) For any given person, *on some particular occasion* during a normal lifetime it is guaranteed that she will sin.

Notice the crucial difference between these two propositions. Both ascribe necessity to the performance of sin. But the latter ascribes the necessity of sinning to some particular occasion, while the former does not. Thus, the scope of the modifier "guaranteed" is different in these propositions. The propositions may be stated more simply as follows (where the term "guaranteed" is replaced by "necessarily"):

(P1') *Necessarily,* every person will sin at some time.

(P2') Every person will at some time *necessarily* sin.

The point of the above argument is to show that P1' implies P2'. If the argument is sound, Christians are mistaken in believing both that everyone will in fact sin and that their so sinning is not by compulsion. So how ought one respond?

The argument is fallacious. The logical error committed here is the fallacy of division. It does not follow from the fact that the whole has a particular property that the same property is possessed by some of the component parts. Consider the analogy of a raffle. Suppose one hundred raffle tickets are sold, and a winner is to be chosen at random. Now for any particular ticket, it is highly unlikely that it will win (the odds are one in one hundred). Yet (assuming a winning ticket is drawn) it is guaranteed that one of the tickets will in fact win. So the necessity of some ticket or other winning does not imply the necessity of any particular ticket winning. (And as regards belief, it is perfectly rational to believe that some ticket or other will win, while in the case of any ticket in particular, disbelieving that it will win.) The modifier "necessarily wins" or "is guaranteed to win" applies not to any raffle ticket in particular. Rather, the necessity applies to the whole collection of raffle tickets.

Similarly, to return to our case of guaranteed sinning, the modifier "necessarily sins" or "is guaranteed to sin" applies to an entire lifetime of choices. The necessity of sinning is not a property of any particular movement of the person's will. But, given the agent's sinful nature, the propensity toward sin is strong enough to ensure that over a normal lifetime of perhaps millions of choices, she will choose sinfully at one time or another. That is to say, it is guaranteed that she will eventually sin. So the Christian can reasonably affirm both that all persons will in fact sin due to their sinful nature and that they do not sin by compulsion. That is to say, it is guaranteed that human beings, because of their sinful nature, will sin, but they do so freely.

My defense of this position has not presupposed a particular view on the freedom-determinism question, but it would presumably be most useful to proponents of "libertarianism," since to hold this view is to base the possibility of human freedom upon the supposition that a free human will does not have a cause (i.e., antecedent conditions sufficient to guarantee an effect, in this case an act of the will). A free will, according to the libertarian, must possess the "power of contrary choice." That is, in the case of, say, possible action X, someone is free if and only if it is causally possible for her to either do or not do X.

I reject the libertarian view of human freedom. The principle of sufficient reason says that there must be some causal explanation for the existence of any being or positive fact whatsoever, and I see no reason why the human will should be an exception to this rule, provided that an adequate account of freedom can be salvaged compatible with this determinism. I believe such an account is possible, which is to say that I am a "compatibilist." A compatibilist defines freedom as the ability to act according to one's choice. On this view, then, the essential question is not whether causal laws prevail in the psychological realm. Rather, the salient issue is whether a person is physically able to act according to her choices. Freedom, on this view, is a property of persons, not wills. So even though the will of a rational agent is caused, principally by such psychological factors as motives, desires, incentives, personal dispositions, and so forth, she is nevertheless free, assuming she can *act* on her choice.

The compatibilist, unlike the libertarian, affirms causal necessity within the mind of the agent. The workings of a sinful nature may necessarily result in some bad actions for which a person is still responsible. For she acts according to her nature, and any choice that a person makes which flows from her own nature is *ipso facto* free, irrespective of the fact that the choice was entirely determined by antecedent causal conditions. What makes a person free or unfree (and therefore responsible or not) is whether there are external forces restraining or compelling the agent in the carrying out of her chosen action.

So the compatibilist affirms while the libertarian denies the causal determination of the will in free human choices, but both affirm the significant freedom of the agent nonetheless. While Christians are divided over the freedom-determinism issue from a metaphysical standpoint, they are agreed that human beings are, generally speaking, morally responsible, however this is properly to be conceived. Both approaches to the freedom-determinism issue are consistent with the orthodox Christian doctrine of original sin and the concomitant conviction that all persons eventually sin in fact.

CAUSES AND CURES OF AKRASIA

We now turn our attention to issues more "existential" in nature. Specifically, what are the natural causes of moral weakness? How might moral weakness be avoided? And to what extent, if at all, is it possible for the *akrates* to be reformed?

Contributing Natural Causes of Akrasia

As if a sinful nature were not enough of an obstacle for fallen human beings to contend with, other factors enter into decision-making that can predispose a person to taking the akratic alternative in difficult choices. Amelie Rorty has identified a number of these, and the discussion that follows depends heavily upon her work.[15]

1. Psychological Causes. Every person possesses a unique combination of cognitive abilities and emotional traits, and so may be particularly prone to akratic behavior because of such endowments. For example, a person with a poor imagination may be more likely to succumb to temptation. As Rorty elaborates, "the preferred good . . . can seem less real to him because he does not know how to specify it in detail, because he can only conceive it schematically."[16] Of course, imaginative weakness may derive from lack of training, genetic predisposition, or some combination thereof. But it seems that anyone, regardless of his or her abilities in this area, can improve.

Also, proneness to extreme emotions, such as fears and phobias, can drive a person toward the akratic choice. As Aristotle observes, human beings tend to err in the direction of the less dangerous of two vices (where virtue is conceived as a mean between two vicious extremes).[17] For example, Peter's cowardice in the courtyard of the high priest was no doubt motivated by fear for his own physical well-being. The cowardly choice was the safer route for him.

2. Social Causes. Intertwined with (and sometimes causally connected to) psychological preconditions of *akrasia* are social forces. Experiences of abuse or other forms of victimization can lead to feelings of powerlessness that diminish one's drive to resist a preferred course of action. Through persistent failure at attempts of self-assertion, a person may become behaviorally conditioned to simply "go with the flow," even in vital matters.

A person may be conditioned by social streaming, as well. If she is consistently typecast as a certain kind of person, she may akratically assume the role, acting as she is "expected" to act, although such behavior goes against her better judgment. Also, the desire to be accepted by one's peers is a powerful force in decision-making. Clark, the akratic alcoholic, may find the temptation to drink overwhelming because of the "social pressure." Or, if unfazed by enticements of social esteem, he may be more readily led astray by the effects of his upbringing, if taking the path of least resistance was a behavior generally reinforced by his parents and siblings.

3. Political Causes. Extreme power, as is wielded by persons of great political clout, not only leads to unique temptations but can also prompt *akrasia*. This occurs, explains Rorty, because such power "allows unusual scope for the akratic release of the powerful but stressed person. The normal checks and constraints that might add weight to the preferred course are absent."[18] This might help to explain the remarkable and tragic indulgences of some politicians and other public figures in recent years. While it might not necessarily be the case that, as Bacon says, "power corrupts," such cases certainly suggest that extreme power does nothing to enhance one's ability to act in accordance with her best judgment.

The Virtue of Self-Control: Avoiding *Akrasia*

The roughly Aristotelian model of *akrasia* that I defended in the previous chapter attributes the phenomenon to a lack of self-control. The *akrates* succumbs to temptation due to a failure to harness certain passions or appetites contradicting his better judgment. Thus, it is said, his moral will is weak. This account suggests an obvious answer as to how moral weakness may be avoided and the *akrates* reformed. The key lies in developing self-control. It is the absence of this virtue which makes *akrasia* possible, so it would stand to reason that its presence is essential to successfully combating moral weakness. What is not so obvious is how this virtue is cultivated.

Moral virtues are character traits developed only through practice. They do not come by mere teaching, as Aristotle correctly argued, but must be nurtured through disciplined training like any other skill or ability. Nor does their full maturation come quickly but only through years of application. This is why Aristotle says that virtue is "always concerned with what is harder."[19] The good life requires the most serious commitment.

Cultivation of self-control has several dimensions. The more attentive one is to each, the greater success he is likely to have in developing self-control. Several useful strategies for increasing self-control have been proposed.

1. Preparatory Strategies. The poet Heinrich Heine once wrote that "the thought precedes the deed as the lightning the thunder." The seeker of the virtue of self-control must purpose his mind toward mastery of his baser impulses. A prerequisite for doing so is moral introspection—increasing self-awareness with special attention to one's own peculiar weaknesses, emotions, drives, and appetites. This is the crucial diagnostic step in the quest for self-control. Knowing the enemy always increases the likelihood of success in battle.

It is also important to practice anticipatory thinking. When appropriate, one should plan to avoid unnecessary exposure to temptation. Of course, successful application of this strategy hinges upon one's moral self-awareness. You must know your specific moral Achilles' heels before you can properly plan to avoid exposing them.[20] Finally, resolution is essential. A person must be intentional in his resolve to be morally strong. This means having some minimal plan or strategy.[21]

2. Mental and Spiritual Disciplines. The training of the mind through the use of meditation is a valuable but often neglected tool for building self-control. One may apply what Amelie Rorty calls "attentive focusing."[22] Here, for example, one intentionally envisions the negative fallout of giving into temptation and contrasts this with the probable benefits of resisting.[23] And dwelling on moral goods or, as Paul says, whatever is noble, right, pure, lovely, excellent, or praiseworthy, is likely to impact one's desires in a positive way.[24]

Prayer is also critical for cultivating self-control. The effectiveness of prayer in this regard is probably due in part to the fact that it involves such elements as mental discipline, positive moral focusing, and, to some extent, the practice of self-denial.

3. Behavioral Disciplines. It is axiomatic for any serious athlete that "practice makes perfect," and, if Aristotle is right, this is no less the case in the moral life.[25] Self-control must be practiced, but one need not wait for morally significant situations to arise to do so. Self-control is a "transferable skill." So to practice it in one area, however trivial, is to improve the skill for all possible areas of application. William James took note of this and advised that one "do every day or two something for no other reason than that you would rather not do it, so that when the hour of dire need draws nigh, it may find you not unnerved and untrained to stand the test."[26] James's practical insight reveals the value of fasting, for example, an especially powerful tool for building self-control, as it involves resistance of one of our strongest drives.[27]

Additionally, the use of positive and negative reinforcement is a long-recognized form of behavioral self-training. Rewarding or punishing oneself for resisting or giving in to temptation can be morally constructive by causing one to associate moral virtue with pleasure and vice with pain. Lastly, constructive expression of negative emotions can relieve stress, anger, and other negative feelings that tempt one to poor behavior. For example, calisthenics, jogging, punching a pillow, or yelling can be helpful in this regard.

4. Self-Trickery. There are also methods by which a person can "trick" herself into acting morally and, in the process, contribute to the development of self-control. One of these is the use of "conflicting behavior therapy," which involves intentionally acting in ways that contradict one's emotions. For example, a person who feels fearful may concentrate on simply appearing courageous. Robert Roberts writes, "I think that courageous people are typically aware, intuitively, of the influence that their bodily dispositions and voice and speech have on their anxiety and fear, and practice this kind of self-management. It is far from obvious that courageous people typically feel fears and anxieties less intensely than cowardly people. But through practice in facing up to threatening situations, they have learned how to manage and mitigate their fears."[28]

Self-commands are also useful for reinforcing self-management. This may take the form of either speaking imperatives to oneself about a present situation (e.g., "Don't do it Jim; you'll only regret it.") or quoting some applicable proverb aloud (e.g., "Fools rush in where angels fear to tread.").

Since the sinful nature seems unscrupulous in its devices to overrun one's better judgment, it is perhaps appropriate to be cleverly deceitful in return. What Robert Roberts calls "hoaxing lust" is an example. He explains how, for instance, a weak-willed gambler may tell himself that he only intends to resist his temptation for a day, after which he again vows abstinence for only another twenty-four hours. Repeated short-term vows of this kind will, if successful, result in an ingrained habit that can harden into a virtuously self-controlled character.[29]

Lastly, in a book titled *Strength of the Will and How to Develop It,* Boyd Barrett suggests a number of "gymnastics" of the will. They include such exercises as the following:

1. Repeat quietly and aloud: "I *will* do *this,*" keeping time with rhythmic movements of a stick or ruler for five minutes.
2. Walk to and fro in a room, touching in turn, say, a clock on the mantelpiece and a particular pane of glass for five minutes.
3. Listen to the ticking of a clock or watch, making some definite movements at every fifth tick.
4. Get up and down from a chair thirty times.

5. Replace in a box, very slowly and deliberately, one hundred matches or bits of paper (an exercise particularly adapted to combat impulsiveness).[30]

Such seemingly useless regimens actually serve to increase one's concentration and stamina, capacities essential for successfully resisting powerful temptations.

Whatever the technique employed, the cultivation of the virtue of self-control is strongly and explicitly endorsed in the Scriptures. It is one of the fruits of the Spirit, says Paul in Galatians 5:22–23. And he tells Timothy that "God did not give us a spirit of timidity, but a spirit of power, of love and of self-discipline."[31] Elsewhere, Peter exhorts us: "Be self-controlled and alert. Your enemy the devil prowls around like a roaring lion looking for someone to devour. Resist him, standing firm in the faith. . . ."[32] Such exhortations remind us that self-control is an essential Christian virtue.

They also remind us that the moral life is difficult, and we are all handicapped in one way or another. The obstacles that face us, such as those discussed earlier, lead Rorty to remark that "a voluntary agent requires Tory habits and Whig critical capacities."[33] Of course, from a Christian point of view, a great deal more than this is necessary for living the good life. It is precisely here that the Scriptures offer "good news" for us sin-tainted humans. The atoning death and resurrection of Jesus Christ provides the opportunity for divine forgiveness for sins (original and actually performed). And on top of this, the Holy Spirit seeks to help improve the repentant sinner in her daily life. Divine assistance is available in the struggle to overcome *akrasia,* which is good news indeed. This process of growth in the virtue of self-control and of ultimately achieving moral strength is an essential part of what theologians call "sanctification."

SANCTIFICATION: REFORMING THE *AKRATES*

Let us look more closely at this theological concept of sanctification. To sanctify is "to make holy" or "to set apart" (*qadas* in Hebrew), and ethically speaking this involves growth in virtue and obedience to divine commands. To grow in sanctification is to increase in likeness to God. The Scriptures speak repeatedly of this moral improvement as the continuing aim of the Christian. And as Jesus asserts, our moral standard is nothing less than divine: "Be perfect . . . as your heavenly Father is perfect."[34] About this much there is consensus among Christian theologians. But on a number of other matters pertaining to the doctrine there is disagreement.

As I see it, four basic views of sanctification have been advanced by Christian theologians. In surveying these, we shall pay special attention to two basic concerns: (1) whether sanctification is a cooperative venture between God and human beings and (2) whether complete sanctification (moral perfection) is possible in this earthly life.

Roman Catholics view sanctification as a concomitant of justification. To be justified necessarily involves inner renewal and the eradication of one's sins. Renewal, the positive effect of justification, is called the "comity of sanctifying grace," whereby moral virtues are actually imparted to the soul.[35] While faith is a precondition for justification, the instrumental causes of justification are the sacraments, which include baptism, confirmation, eucharist, penance, extreme unction, holy orders, and marriage. They are therefore referred to as the "means of grace," as opposed to mere symbols of spiritual realities. According to Catholicism, then, the Christian's justification before God consists in infused righteousness, as opposed to the Protestant idea of imputed righteousness. This is not to say that a Christian achieves a state of moral perfection. In fact, purgatory (postmortem suffering) may be necessary for the complete cleansing of sin to prepare the believer for her heavenly existence.[36]

As is apparent in their emphasis on sacramental rites, Roman Catholics regard sanctification as a work to which human beings vitally contribute. Moreover, they do not really distinguish between the process of growth in personal holiness and justification. Protestant perspectives, on the other hand, sharply distinguish between them. Sanctification, they maintain, is a lifelong process, while justification is a finished work for every believer. Thus, the Christian enjoys the status of righteousness, though she does not yet possess the nature of righteousness. The latter is promised the Christian but is not achieved until glorification in heaven. These two senses of righteousness correspond to the two senses of original sin inherited by humans: guilt and pollution. To be justified is to have one's guilt removed, and to be sanctified is to have the pollution of sin removed.[37]

Since the Scriptures sometimes speak of sanctification as already complete for the Christian, some Reformed theologians distinguish between "definitive" and "progressive" sanctification. The former term refers to the Christian's decisive break with sin at the time of conversion, while the latter refers to the progressive renewal in grace and increasing Christ-likeness experienced by the believer after conversion. In either case, the work of sanctification is God's. Of course, human beings are responsible to participate in this ongoing moral transformation, but the source of strength in the process is the Holy Spirit who sovereignly works in the believer to will and act according to God's commands.[38]

Dispensationalists, too, deny that the Christian can achieve "ultimate" moral perfection here on earth.[39] However, a "relative" degree of perfection is possible, whereby a person can "manifest godliness in a significant way."[40] Where dispensational and Reformed theologians differ regards the extent to which human beings can be said to participate in their sanctification. Dispensationalists maintain that the Christian plays a significant causal role in the sanctifying process, which Reformed theologians deny.[41]

The Wesleyan perspective is allied with the dispensational view in recognizing believers as significant agents in their own sanctification. In fact, Wesleyans tend to emphasize this point, though they do not go so far as Roman Catholics. What distinguishes Wesleyans from dispensationalists is their optimism about the degree of sanctification a person can achieve in this life. While John Wesley himself held that no one, "while he is in a corruptible body, can attain to Adamic perfection,"[42] he did believe it possible for the Christian to be freed from all "voluntary transgressions" of the law of God.[43] And other theologians in the Wesleyan tradition have affirmed that such "entire sanctification" is possible. For example, some Assemblies of God and Keswickian writers hold that through the work of the Holy Spirit the Christian is "able not to sin."[44] That is, according to this view, it is possible to live a life of consistent victory over sin. However, the Wesleyan definition of sin here is restricted to intentional transgression of the known law of God. So as optimistic as these theologians are regarding the prospects of moral improvement for the Christian, even they do not claim that a state of absolute moral perfection is possible on this side of paradise.

Thus, the four theological camps reviewed above differ in some important ways, such as regarding the degree of moral improvement possible for the Christian and the question of causal agency in the process of sanctification. But they are united in affirming that complete sinlessness can never be attained in this life. It is easy to see why there is such unanimity on this matter, given the biblical evidence. Such passages as 2 Chronicles 6:36; Psalm 14:1–3; Proverbs 20:9; Ecclesiastes 7:20; James 3:2; and 1 John 1:8 confirm that all human beings sin. Even the greatest of biblical saints are depicted as admitting their sinfulness before God (Psalm 32:4–5; Isaiah 64:6–7; Daniel 9:16; and Romans 7:14–25). And the Christian life is characterized in the Scripture as one of constant struggle with sin (Gal. 5:16–17). In this battle even the mature apostle Paul admitted he had not achieved perfection (Phil. 3:12–14). It is no wonder that the possibility of absolute moral perfection is rejected by all mainline theological traditions of the Christian church.

CONCLUSION

The causes of moral weakness or *akrasia* are various. Human beings not only have original sin to contend with in striving to live the good life, there are numerous "natural" causes which serve as further obstacles. In our moral struggle, therefore, the development of the virtue of self-control is essential. Since a moral virtue is a skill or ability of a certain kind, deliberate training to enhance one's self-control is appropriate, and many strategies can be helpful toward this end. Improvement in this area builds moral strength and, thus, the ability to combat *akrasia*. Sanctification is the theological term for the process of moral improvement or growth in godliness. While Christians have taken a wide range of perspectives on the precise nature of this process, there is uniformity of opinion among mainline theological camps that a state of absolute moral perfection cannot be attained by the Christian in this life.

Cheating at the Goodness Stakes

A Moral Analysis of Hypocrisy

Hypocrisy is the homage vice pays to virtue.
> Francois de La Rochefoucauld

Only the hypocrite is really rotten to the core.
> Hannah Arendt

While it is clear from the Scriptures—especially Jesus' treatment of the Pharisees—that hypocrisy is morally wrong, it is not clear from the Bible exactly why it is wrong. In this chapter we shall address this question. This will be no easy task, for hypocrisy is a complex phenomenon, sometimes resulting from self-deception and at other times revealing a lack of moral seriousness. Another fact that complicates our investigation is that there is no general consensus as to what is "the" biblical ethical theoretical framework. Therefore, before beginning a moral analysis of hypocrisy, we must first address this philosophical issue.

THREE MAJOR MORAL TRADITIONS

"Metaethics" is that branch of moral philosophy which inquires into the nature of ethical theories and the meaning of moral judgments and terms. What do such statements as "X is good" mean? What do the terms "obligation," "virtue," and "sin" denote? And which moral theory, if any, is correct? These are the questions that fall into the domain of metaethical inquiry. And they must be answered before one can move on to consider issues in "normative ethics," which pertains to the rightness or wrongness of particular acts such as hypocrisy.

For the Christian moral philosopher metaethical inquiry must be informed by the Bible, for it is God's special revelation to us regarding, among other things, how we ought to live. Granting this much, though, biblical ethicists and Christian philosophers disagree over which moral paradigm best "fits" the biblical data. This is a complex and difficult debate that will not be settled here. In the interest of being ecumenical, it will be best simply to review the moral theories which, from a historical standpoint anyway, are the most important.

Three basic orientations have been taken in the history of metaethics, and any moral theory may be categorized as falling into one of these camps: teleological, deontological, or virtue ethics. Teleological theories emphasize the purpose or goal of actions.[1] An act is right or wrong depending upon its actual or probable consequences. Deontological theories deemphasize consequences and focus instead on the concept of duty. To be moral, essentially, is to meet one's obligations. Finally, the tradition of virtue ethics concentrates on moral qualities, habits, or dispositions. The emphasis is not actions so much as persons. To be moral is to be a certain kind of person with a particular set of character traits.

Corresponding to these three distinct emphases in ethics are three immensely influential philosophical traditions, specifically utilitarian, Kantian, and Aristotelian ethics.

106

Utilitarian-Teleological Ethics

According to utilitarian ethics, the only intrinsic good is pleasure. It is the end of all our actions and the only thing desirable in itself. The rightness or wrongness of any action is therefore properly evaluated by its potential for producing pleasure. Nineteenth-century British philosopher John Stuart Mill offered this definition of basic moral concepts: "Actions are right in proportion as they tend to promote happiness, wrong as they tend to produce the reverse of happiness. By happiness is intended pleasure, and the absence of pain; by unhappiness, pain and the privation of pleasure."[2] While formalized into a systematic ethical theory by Mill and his mentor Jeremy Bentham, the roots of moral hedonism are almost as ancient as philosophy itself, the Epicurean school of ancient Greek philosophy being the most notable advocate of this idea.[3]

Bentham proposed that moral analysis should proceed by applying what he calls a "hedonic calculus," in which a particular action or state of affairs is evaluated by its probable long-term consequences.[4] If it is determined that the act in question is likely to produce more pleasure than pain, it is a good act. If pain is likely to prevail, it is wrong.

While affirming Bentham's basic hedonism, Mill qualified his position in a short but influential work titled *Utilitarianism,* noting that not all pleasures are qualitatively equal. Some pleasures are intrinsically "higher" than others. These higher pleasures include those of which only human beings are capable, such as those that are intellectual and emotional in nature. Hence, as Mill tells us, human misery is morally superior to even the highest degree of brute pleasures, precisely because we enjoy such greater capacities. "It is better to be a human being dissatisfied than a pig satisfied; better to be Socrates dissatisfied than a fool satisfied."[5]

Mill also clarified some points of utilitarianism in response to some common criticisms. For instance, many have objected that the pleasure-pain calculus is too difficult. How can we reliably predict the consequences of a particular act? Human beings are not omniscient, and much of the future seems, even probabilistically, impossible to anticipate. Mill's apt reply is that we can base our judgments on what we have learned from the past. During all human history, "mankind have been learning by experience the tendencies of actions on which experience all the prudence as well as all the morality of life are dependent."[6] And to those who would object that his is a "godless doctrine," Mill replies that on the contrary utilitarianism fits perfectly with any religious perspective that believes God desires the happiness of his creatures. Mill's ethics matches especially well with the Christian faith, he says, for "in the golden rule of Jesus of Nazareth, we read the complete spirit of the ethics of utility."[7]

Kantian-Deontological Ethics

Immanuel Kant was an eighteenth-century German philosopher and a prominent figure in the Enlightenment. With such thinkers as Rousseau, Bayle, and Voltaire, he led the movement to free human thought from what he called "self-incurred tutelage," especially oppressive church authority, and to recognize the autonomy of reason on issues ranging from science to faith.[8] In the domain of morality, Kant was convinced that questions of right and wrong, duty and obligation could be decisively answered by appealing to reason, without any explicit reference to God or specific biblical texts.

According to Kant, there is only one unqualified good, and that is a good will. "Intelligence, wit, judgment, and the other talents of the mind . . . are doubtless in many respects good and desirable. But they can become extremely bad and harmful if the will . . . is not good."[9] A good will is characterized not by its effects but by the fact that its choices are determined by a sense of duty.

So just what is our duty? Kant observed that when it comes to matters of fact, there is a supreme logical principle, the law of noncontradiction, which governs rational thought. No proposition can be true that is self-contradictory or cannot be consistently maintained, for example, "Some squares are circles." Similarly, any statement that cannot be rejected without contradiction must be true, for example, "All triangles are three-sided." The law of noncontradiction, then, is a logical imperative, binding on all rational persons. Moreover, it is *a priori,* known independently of experience. It is the foundation of all logical proofs, not something that is itself proven.

It was Kant's thesis that just as there is a supreme logical principle, there is a supreme moral principle that is also known *a priori* and which is binding upon all rational persons. He called this the categorical imperative, for it is a command that applies to all persons without exception. Just as any truth claim regarding a matter of fact must satisfy the law of noncontradiction, all moral propositions must satisfy the categorical imperative. Both demand consistency and forbid contradiction. The only difference is that in the latter case the subject is the human will rather than the understanding; the actions we perform, not the things we believe.

The categorical imperative, Kant maintained, may be formulated in various ways. For instance, it may be stated, "Act only according to that maxim by which you can at the same time will that it should become a universal law."[10] That is, regarding any act, one should only perform it if she could consistently will that all persons everywhere were required to perform it. Thus, such actions as chewing gum, telling jokes, and playing baseball would be permissible (though not obligatory) because one could indeed consistently will that they be performed by all persons. Such actions as suicide, thievery, and slanderous talk, however, would not pass this test. For while one might prefer to steal something on a particular occasion, it would be impossible to will consistently that everyone do so. The reasonable conclusion, then, is that these latter actions are morally prohibitive, while the former are not. Thus, Kant tells us, with regard to any action whatsoever, we will gain proper moral guidance if we but ask, Could I will that a rule to perform this action be made into a universal law? If so, it is permissible. If not, it is wrong.

The categorical imperative may also be expressed in terms of human autonomy and the principle of respect for persons. As Kant articulates it, "Act so that you treat humanity, whether in your own person or in that of another, always as an end and never as a means only."[11] Rational persons are ends in themselves, and our autonomy demands that we be treated as such. So while we may use someone, such as a department store clerk, as a means to our own end, this must not be our sole intent. We must also treat him with dignity and respect. Moreover, we have a duty to respect ourselves as ends. This rules out as immoral such actions as self-harm and suicide.[12]

Aristotelian-Virtue Ethics

The whole approach to morality by the ancient Greeks was different from that of the modern philosophers and contemporary thinkers. Rather than concentrating on such concepts as duty, rights, and rules, as we do today, thinkers such as Plato and Aristotle preferred to focus moral inquiry on persons and character traits. The ultimate human good, Aristotle taught, is happiness, but not conceived primarily as pleasure, as the utilitarians would later define it. Rather, to be happy *(eudaimonia)* is to live well or generally to fulfill one's function as an essentially rational being. That is to say, the contemplative life is the happiest.

According to Aristotle, every human excellence necessarily involves the proper exercise of reason. Virtue is a particular kind of human excellence, which he defines as a habit or trained faculty "which makes a man good and which makes him do his own work well."[13] Now, human beings are not naturally virtuous, Aristotle maintained, but rather become virtuous by engaging in virtuous actions. The performance of virtuous actions becomes habitual through practice and eventually settles into a virtuous character. But what are the sorts of traits that Aristotle would label virtuous? And how are virtues to be distinguished from vices?

Here Aristotle introduces his famous doctrine of the "golden mean." When it comes to any action, there are two ways to err. One may exceed or fall short of the mark. Virtue is, as it were, a mean between extremes. Thus, for example, when it comes to acting in the face of danger, one may fail to act altogether and thus be guilty of the vice of cowardice. On the opposite end, one may rush headlong into danger without caution, which is foolhardy. The virtue lies between the vicious extremes of cowardice and foolhardiness, and this is courage. Similarly, one may overindulge in pleasure or be absolutely insensible, both of which are vices. Moral excellence in the matter of pleasure is temperance. One must display generosity, rather than stinginess or prodigality. One must be modest, not sheepish or shameless. And so it goes for all of the virtues on Aristotle's account. The virtue is always to be found between extremes.

Aristotle's ethics is teleological, but it is not consequentialist as utilitarianism is. It is teleological in the sense that virtue is defined in terms of the *telos* of a person and his community. It is always in light of some role or function that a person serves within a social context that the full set of virtues appropriate to him must be determined. We thus ask regarding a person the same sorts of questions that we ask of any object in discovering its specific "good." Just as a "good" cup is one which fulfills its function in holding liquids, a virtuous physician is one who fulfills her function in restoring health; a virtuous pilot realizes his end of flying his plane safely to its destination; and so on.[14]

THE CHRISTIAN METAETHICAL BALANCE

None of these three major moral traditions depends upon theism, nor presupposes any belief in the reality or even possibility of special divine revelation. In this sense, each of these traditions is essentially secular. But this is not to say that they are essentially atheistic. They are all simply neutral as to questions of the truth of theism, divine revelation, and religious belief. This is why it remains an open question for metaethicists as to which, if any, represents a satisfactory account, in part or in full, of biblical morality. Since the Scriptures are not perfectly explicit as to why God commands this and prohibits that, we must turn to extrabiblical, philosophical explanations to fill in the theoretical gaps (just as we do in other disciplines, such as science, history, economics, etc.).

In attempting to make sense of the biblical data on moral issues, Christian ethicists have come to divergent conclusions as to which metaethical framework best fits the Scriptures. There are Christian utilitarians, Christian Kantians, and Christian Aristotelians, each insisting that the particular theory they favor captures the essence of a truly biblical ethic. Still others insist that while the Scriptures provide guidelines for human conduct, they do not speak at all to theoretical questions regarding why an act is morally good or bad, or exactly what the concepts of a duty or right entail.

The remainder of this chapter will subject the phenomenon of hypocrisy to a moral analysis from the perspective of each of the three major ethical theories. Why all three? First, because it is conceivable to me that any of these three moral frameworks may be the correct one, that is, the ethical theory that best captures the essence of the biblical perspective on moral matters. So to approach the subject of hypocrisy from the standpoint of just one of these theories would be to risk missing out on important moral insights.

Second, this approach reflects my own eclectic position on Christian ethics. I am convinced that each of the three major moral traditions captures at least part of the essence of a biblical, Christian morality. That is, each of the major moral theories can be seen as a truncation of a full-orbed biblical ethic.[15] The utilitarian-teleological tradition focuses on the goal of Christian ethics, namely happiness. And it emphasizes consequences of actions, one very important consideration in moral decision-making. The Kantian-deontological tradition highlights the biblical concept of duty, especially as represented in the divine commands we find in Scripture.[16] Finally, the Aristotelian-virtue ethics tradition stresses the social dynamic of Christian ethics, recognizing the significance of community in defining virtue.

A complete Christian ethic acknowledges the importance of a variety of considerations in evaluating human conduct, and the major moral traditions each seem to place a special accent on one of these. So it should be helpful, even from a specifically Christian perspective, to see what each of these moral traditions has to say about the vice of hypocrisy.

WHY HYPOCRISY IS MORALLY WRONG

Utilitarian-Teleological Ethics

When morally assessing an action, the issue of first importance for the utilitarian is what consequences follow from it. If hypocrisy is morally wrong, what are its negative results?

One of the most famous condemnations of hypocrisy arising from self-deception comes from Father Zossima in Dostoevski's *The Brothers Karamazov*. Zossima warns,

> Above all, don't lie to yourself. The man who lies to himself and listens to his own lie comes to such a pass that he cannot distinguish the truth within him, or around him, and so loses all respect for himself and for others. And having no respect he ceases to love, and in order to occupy and distract himself without love he gives way to passions and coarse pleasures, and sinks to bestiality in his vices, all from continual lying to other men and to himself. The man who lies to himself can be more easily offended than any one. You know it is sometimes very pleasant to take offence, isn't it? A man may know that nobody has insulted him, but that he has invented the insult for himself, has lied and exaggerated to make it picturesque, has caught at a word and made a mountain out of a molehill—he knows that himself, yet he will be the first to take offence, and will revel in his resentment till he feels great pleasure in it, and so pass to genuine vindictiveness. . . . All this, too, is deceitful posturing. . . ."[17]

Here Zossima reviews an alleged domino effect of self-deception. Lying to oneself leads to the loss of ability to discern truth, which erodes self-respect and respect for others, and this diminishes one's ability to love, which finally opens the door to all sorts of vices. So according to Father Zossima and probably Dostoevski himself (since the author represents Zossima as a respectable and wise man of God), there is a causal slippery slope from the hypocrisy of self-deception to the most vile deeds. If this is so, then hypocrisy might be the most dangerous vice of all, for it is potentially the mother of all other vices.

In addition to the effects of self-deception on the hypocrite herself, what specific effects does hypocrisy (whether due to self-deception or lack of moral seriousness) have on other people? First, hypocrisy is annoying to the morally serious, those who work hard to be moral. As has been noted, the hypocrite is, in a sense, a moral thief. She gains approbation by only seeming to be consistently moral. This can kill moral inspiration, for why work hard to get what you can steal?

Second, hypocrisy might be condemnable because of the fear it inspires. As is noted by both Christine McKinnon and Piers Benn, the hypocrite proves herself untrustworthy by being a moral free-rider and not showing proper regard for moral standards. Hence, she represents a threat to those of us who are genuinely concerned about respecting moral ideals. For many, if not most, of us, the reason we refrain from indulging in illicit behavior is that it contradicts certain moral rules we take to be universally binding. Thus, the hypocrite inspires uneasiness, even fear, because she neither respects nor plays by the rules, and her duplicity mocks the very basis of the moral life which we regard both as essential for a meaningful existence and in certain respects as a safeguard against injury.

Fran, from the case study in chapter 2, is a disturbing character not merely because she is biting and caustic but because she knowingly flouts basic moral ideals (e.g., patience, kindness, respect for others). In learning of her hypocrisy, we might ask ourselves, if only subconsciously, "If she is capable of such disregard for moral principles, then what else is she liable to do?" Not surprisingly, we tend to steer clear of such people.

A further negative repercussion of hypocrisy pertains to the potential for harm of the moral community. The exposure of hypocrisy tends to discredit the preaching of the hypocrite which in turn does harm to moral ideals. This harms the moral community generally as people lose their respect for cherished values. Repeated hypocrisies may even have the effect of inclining people toward cynicism and moral skepticism. Erin, the avowed vegetarian, undermines her credibility by eating hamburgers and in the process strains our credulity regarding her cause. And the preacher caught in adultery casts a pall over even his most well-reasoned moral claims.

I make this as a psychological rather than a logical point. To reject any truth claim, be it scientific, metaphysical, or moral, because of who or where it comes from is to commit a logical error known as the "genetic fallacy." The simple fact is that a claim can be true even though it is defended by a maniac; on the other hand, a falsehood can be propounded by a sage. So when an advocate of a particular doctrine acts contrary to it, the truth (if it is truth) itself need not be rejected. Nevertheless, it also seems to be a plain fact of human psychology that our evaluations of those who make truth claims often impact our judgments as much as the truth claims themselves. We must take this into account when making a utilitarian assessment of hypocrisy. If to a substantial segment of the moral community hypocrisy *seems* to undermine moral ideals—to the extent that some moral skepticism results—then the ideals in fact are undermined. In this context perception is fact, a fact which has negative moral value and argues against the moral legitimacy of hypocrisy.

These negative effects of hypocrisy all assume that hypocrisy is revealed for what it is. But what of the secretive hypocrite? Is it not possible that a careful hypocrite could achieve long-term success in her duplicity? In such a case, hypocrisy may inspire others to moral living (as was noted in chapter 2). Just to create the impression that one is righteous can potentially have the same effect on bystanders as a genuinely virtuous life. This undoubtedly is a good consequence.

Erin, the avowed vegetarian, for example, could inspire others to enlist their services in the animal rights movement by her preaching alone. She might even convince people to adopt the eating habits she pretends to model. Similarly, the preacher who warns of the dangers of sexual sin may effectively dissuade others from indulging, in spite of his own secret liaisons.

So hypocrisy may have social benefits, and this presents a problem for the utilitarian ethicist. Consider Erin again. Suppose she is a devout utilitarian who makes her most important moral decisions according to the principle of utility. While on the road during one of her speaking tours she develops a strong appetite for a hamburger. It is a sustained desire but not overwhelming. Though fully convinced that eating meat would violate her moral convictions about animal rights, she weighs the consequences of her potential action of eating the hamburger. "Since no one around here knows who I am," she reasons, "no harm to my cause will result if I indulge. Besides, I am strong enough to keep this from becoming a habit. I will enjoy the burger, and it won't hurt anyone, since it's only one small burger." Erin, then, fulfills the requirements for being the "successful hypocrite." The inconsistency between her teaching and her actions may be discovered by no one. The resulting balance of pleasure over pain would seem to dictate that her temporary deviation from a vegetarian diet is at least morally permissible, if not advisable.

This is a troubling scenario for utilitarian moral theory and might in fact constitute a *reductio ad absurdum* for a consequentialist approach. In fact, this problem resembles another traditional critique of utilitarian theory, that of the voyeur. If a "peeping tom" could be reasonably certain that he would get away with his violation of the privacy of others, then there seems to be no good reason from a utilitarian perspective why he should not do so. Of course, the question in both of these cases is whether we can reasonably expect the "successful" hypocrite or voyeur to stop his behavior or whether it is likely that success will only encourage more indulgence until inevitably the hypocrite or voyeur is caught, at which time negative effects are likely to result.

Some have argued that the only thing that discourages indulgence in vice is the prospect of getting caught. Plato considered just this question in *The Republic*. There Glaucon offers a thought experiment regarding the mythological "ring of Gyges," which has the power to make its possessor invisible, enabling him to do whatever he wants with impunity. If such a ring really existed, Glaucon says, "no one could be found . . . of such adamantine temper as to persevere in justice and endure to refrain his hands from the possessions of others and not touch them . . . and enter into houses and lie with whom he pleased, and slay and loose from bonds whomsoever he would, and in all other things conduct himself among mankind as the equal of a god."[18] Glaucon's point is that "no one is just of his own will but only from constraint, in the belief that justice is not his personal good, inasmuch as every man, when he supposes himself to have the power to do wrong, does wrong."[19]

Is Glaucon's thesis correct? This is an open question, not easily answered. In the dialogue, Socrates remains unpersuaded by Glaucon and argues that the moral life is also the most beneficial. But this does not undermine Glaucon's basic contention, that so long as a person thinks that an immoral act is in his best interest, he will do it, if he is confident he will get away with it. If Glaucon's position is right, then there really is no reason to think that the hypocrite will eventually desist in his vice. Perhaps the real question is whether his successes will necessarily make him careless, as is often the case with serial criminals. If not, there might be no reason for the would-be hypocrite to avoid hypocrisy, assuming he maintains his pretense with great care and skill.

It seems that based solely on the effects of the hypocrite's behavior on others, the utilitarian cannot conclusively condemn hypocrisy. The best consequentialist tack would probably be to take a Dostoevskian approach and build the case against hypocrisy on the likely ill-effects of self-deception on the hypocrite himself. From there one can reason to further likely negative effects on others as the moral spirit of the hypocrite is deadened.[20]

Kantian-Deontological Ethics

From a Kantian perspective, hypocrisy must be evaluated not for its utility in producing pleasure but rather on the basis of (1) whether it arises from a good will, (2) whether it can be universalized, and (3) whether it is respectful of persons, treating them as ends.

First, we must inquire, is hypocrisy necessarily performed with bad motives, a lack of good will? Despite initial appearances to the contrary, we realize that Tartuffe is not really humble, once his actual motives to weasel himself into the good graces of Orgon come to light. The same goes for the Pharisees, about whom the gospel writers say, "Jesus knew their thoughts," that is, their real intentions. In cases such as these, a bad will makes behavior that initially appears virtuous turn out to be quite the opposite.

For the Kantian, it is true by definition that the actions of the hypocrite who is not morally serious do not arise from a good will, for a good will is one whose motive is specifically to abide by the moral law. The "amoral" hypocrite does not even satisfy the first prerequisite of a good will, namely acknowledgment that there is a moral law that applies to her. Thus, her pretense is really double, for she feigns (1) recognition of a moral law and (2) that she abides by the moral law.

The hallmarks of these hypocrites are their selfishness and insincerity. These characteristics are definitive of hypocrisy, as some contemporary philosophers have pointed out. Christine McKinnon has noted that "in the purest example of the true hypocrite the correct explanation for her behavior is simply a desire to mislead those who judge her, usually in order to gain some further good for herself."[21] In a similar vein, Eva Kittay says that "lack of sincerity is . . . precisely what makes hypocrisy morally blameworthy in those cases where the hypocrisy is blameworthy. . . . This is because the hypocrite . . . is insincere in just those domains where sincerity really matters—such as piety, virtue, love and friendship."[22]

It is for this reason, Kittay adds, that a thoroughgoing consequentialist ethic cannot account for the blameworthiness of hypocrisy. A metaethical framework that focuses upon actions and excludes consideration of intentions when making moral judgments must simply ignore hypocrisy as morally irrelevant.

Now what about the second Kantian criterion for moral actions? Does the hypocrite treat persons as ends in themselves and never as means only? Clearly not. Uriah Heep denied his financial aspirations specifically so he could bilk Mr. Wickfield. The Pharisees' hypocrisy was disrespectful of persons because they used their deception to saddle others with an unnecessary moral burden. In fact, every case of hypocrisy, by definition of the vice, fundamentally involves deception of some kind that is in the immediate interest of the hypocrite alone. The person deceived is often harmed by the deceit or by the subsequent deeds the hypocrite is enabled to perform through his ruse.

When hypocrisy involves self-deception it would seem to be doubly wrong from the standpoint of respect for persons. In such cases the hypocrite not only treats others as mere means, she disrespects herself. The self-deceiver is guilty of the same moral vice that the plain liar is. She fails to treat someone, namely herself, as an end. As for the amoral hypocrite, she does not merely disobey the categorical imperative; she flouts it. In doing so, she is not merely immoral but irrational as well, since in Kant's view morality is an aspect of rationality. To be a hypocrite of this kind is to tacitly deny one's rational nature, that aspect of human beings that constitutes our personhood and distinguishes us from the brutes. Therefore, "amoral" hypocrisy is fundamentally self-degrading, a basic disrespecting of oneself.

Furthermore, the second-order hypocrite forsakes the very preconditions of the good life. And as Crisp and Cowton note, "if anything is morally blameworthy, then lack of concern for morality itself surely is."[23] The hypocrite is a moral impostor, who creates a facade of a moralist while actually denying the moral constraints acknowledged by genuine members of the moral community, thus sabotaging the very essence of morality.[24]

When we apply the criterion of universalizability, hypocrisy is condemned on several counts. First, hypocrisy of either kind involves deception of others. And a maxim to deceive others could never be consistently willed to be a universal law, for all persons desire sincerity from others. Moreover, such a maxim would undermine all trust, and all of us want to be trusted, even the hypocrite.

Self-deception violates this version of the categorical imperative for similar reasons. If self-deception became normative, this would result in the same sort of moral chaos that universal deception of others would. No one could trust anyone else. But on top of this, no one could ever trust himself!

Hypocrisy as a lack of moral seriousness could never be universalized, because it would constitute the end of morality. If no one were morally serious, then there would be moral anarchy, which no one could consistently will, not even the amoral hypocrite. Notice that in such a world hypocrisy itself would be impossible, for a generally acknowledged and respected moral law is necessary to create the possibility for a pretense of moral righteousness. Of course, the end of all hypocrisy is in itself a desirable thing but would only come at the greatest possible cost—the loss of morality itself.

Aristotelian-Virtue Ethics

From the perspective of Aristotelian-virtue ethics, actions are evaluated according to whether they are conducive to or befitting a virtuous character. And a virtue is any quality that makes a person a "good specimen" within her community.[25] For any trait that is considered vicious, there is some corresponding virtue that it opposes. So the question the Aristotelian must ask is, Which virtue (or set of virtues) does hypocrisy oppose?

Several possibilities come to mind. Consider first the virtue of honesty or truthfulness. As Thomas Aquinas notes, "hypocrisy is a lie told by outward deeds."[26] Like any liar in the usual sense, the hypocrite deliberately creates a false impression about himself or some state of affairs that works to his favor. Tartuffe's elaborate prayers hid the truth about his real ambitions. Judge Pyncheon's politeness and social graces did not express his true nature. So their hypocrisy can certainly be seen as antithetical to honesty.

A problem arises here as we apply this reasoning to common courtesies where for various reasons we put up a front to create an impression that is not quite reflective of the truth. If we should always be truthful with our actions, then is it morally wrong to give a cheerful greeting to persons we find annoying, offensive, or whom we otherwise do not like?[27] And is it ethically questionable to pretend to be feeling better than we are when we feel a sickness coming on? Such behavior, like any hypocrisy of pretense, is less than honest about our true attitude or condition, so is it therefore wrong? If not, then what is the difference between such cases and the "dishonest" behavior of a Tartuffe or Pyncheon? In short, I think the key difference lies in the intention of the deceiver. The person who is deceptively kind or who creates a false impression of perfect health usually does so for the sake of others rather than solely for her own benefit. That is to say, such deception is not entirely selfish as is the hypocrite's. Another important factor has to do with practicality. In some social situations it would be awkward, perhaps even rude, to show one's true feelings about another person, be they negative or positive (in, say, a romantic sense). The hypocrite, on the other hand, can appeal to no such mitigating factors to justify her deceit. Her behavior is prompted neither by practicality nor altruistic ends.

Another virtue opposing hypocrisy is justice. A just person gives to each her proper due and is fair in exchanges of goods, including praise and blame. Some hypocrisies involve avoidance of penalty for one's morally offensive actions. David is an excellent example. Though his action deserved the same condemnation he gave the man in Nathan's parable, he overlooked his own sin. Saul's violation of the very laws he made and was supposed to enforce went unpunished. In other cases, the hypocrite receives credit for no good reason. Judge Pyncheon received credit for his apparent good will. And Tartuffe was rewarded for his superficial humility. As Piers Benn notes, "A hypocrite is a kind of free-rider. He gets respect without contributing the effort which such respect is normally based upon, and whilst maintaining the importance of such an effort by others."[28]

This also helps to explain our antipathy for hypocritical behavior. In the words of Christine McKinnon, "we dislike the hypocrite because we feel she is somehow cheating at the 'goodness stakes.' She is collecting unwarranted moral kudos or avoiding merited blame and we resent her for that."[29] Not only does this approach explain why hypocrisy is condemned; it also explains why other forms of deception, such as pretending to be less virtuous than one is, are not. In this case no undue moral credit is reaped; nor is justifiable blame avoided.

The virtue of conscientiousness is another possibility. This is the trait exhibited by those who take their moral obligations seriously. Clearly, on this score the hypocrite fails miserably. The form of hypocrisy involving lack of moral seriousness distinguishes itself by this very fault. Erin, for instance, utterly disregards the dietary implications of her strong animal rights position. And the self-deceived hypocrite labors under the delusion that her actions are righteous while in reality she is no more conscientious than the other sort of hypocrite. The Pharisees provide a good example. Their lack of conscientiousness is shown repeatedly in the gospel narratives, as they preoccupy themselves with petty disputes and neglect the weightier matters of the moral law.

Integrity is another virtue opposed by hypocrisy. This virtue applies to the person whose moral life is consistent. She is a person who walks her talk, practices what she preaches, and does so steadfastly. Integrity is in one sense the moral equivalent of logical consistency. But as legal and moral philosopher Ronald Dworkin notes, it is more than mere consistency.[30] It implies a sort of coherence about one's life. To be a person of integrity is to act in such a way that one's words and deeds are naturally seen as flowing from a single mind.[31] The hypocrite, however, engages in actions which most emphatically do not cohere with her words or her other actions. Fran, for instance, is polite to the viewing public but spiteful to her staff. This lack of integrity is precisely what prompts us to call her "double-minded."

A final virtue opposed by hypocrisy is civic-mindedness. The civic-minded person deliberates with the welfare of his community in view. He recognizes that his own good is tied up not only with that of his family but his society as well. Therefore, any act prompted by purely selfish motives is vicious, because it is antithetical—or at least indifferent—to the ends and interests of the broader community in which he lives. Hypocrisy is necessarily selfishly motivated (or in Kantian terms, it treats others as mere means, as we saw earlier). So it is not civic-minded.

To these general virtues opposed by hypocrisy, we might add to our Aristotelian analysis a consideration of virtues that are project- or role-specific. There are many tasks or vocations which could never be properly fulfilled by someone who indulges in hypocrisy. Teachers and preachers of all kinds, for instance, must act consistently with their instruction or they undermine their livelihood. Those who fail to practice what they preach or teach are incredible as well as annoying. Law enforcement personnel and other public officials must abide by the laws they enforce lest their authority be undermined. And then there are countless other professionals such as merchants, bankers, physicians, and skilled craftsmen whose success demands the trust of their customers, a trust which hypocrisy naturally destroys.

WHY HYPOCRITES ARE ESPECIALLY DESPISED

Why are hypocrites so strongly despised? Why do we some-times hear people say things like, "I may do such and such, but at least I am not a hypocrite," as if to imply that there is no worse moral fate than to be guilty of hypocrisy? I believe it is because this vice is wrong at so many levels:

1. Hypocrisy is a form of deception, specifically a kind of dishonesty in which a person lies by deeds.
2. Hypocrisy is insincere and disrespectful of persons.
3. Hypocrisy is unjust, as it involves moral free-loading and the hypocrite unfairly receives goods as a result.
4. Hypocrisy kills the moral spirit by undermining the incentive to live morally.
5. Hypocrisy flouts morality itself at its foundation.

The vice of hypocrisy is hydra-headed, many sins in one. This justifies the extreme repugnance it provokes and our strong resistance to being accused of hypocrisy. It is in many ways the worst of vices.[32] Hannah Arendt echoes this judg-ment: "What makes it so plausible to assume that hypocrisy is the vice of vices is that integrity can indeed exist under the cover of all other vices except this one. Only crime and the criminal, it is true, confront us with the perplexity of radical evil; but only the hypocrite is really rotten to the core."[33]

HYPOCRISY AND RESPECT FOR THE MORAL LAW

It has been said that "hypocrisy is the homage vice pays to virtue."[34] This point, ironic though it is, should not be missed. An amoralist may deny that there is an objective moral code which obligates her to perform certain actions and refrain from others, but it is difficult to live out this sort of moral skep-ticism. As C. S. Lewis notes, even the most relativistic among us will betray her inner conviction that there are absolute val-ues. It is evidenced in the way people talk about values and hold one another responsible for their actions.[35] Hypocrisy sometimes is motivated by this same tendency to acknowledge the moral law, whether in word or deed.

Hypocrisy might in fact evidence a sense of divinity within even the most depraved. John Calvin argues along these lines, maintaining that because of the majesty of God which persistently weighs upon the hearts of unbelievers, they perform "some semblance of religion," all the while indulging in various sins. According to Calvin, the result is hypocrisy, at once the worst of vices and a sign of a divine sense in the darkest of human hearts. Of hypocrites he says,

> Where they ought to serve [God] in sanctity of life and integrity of heart, they trump up frivolous trifles and worthless little observances with which to win his favor. Nay, more, with greater license they sluggishly lie in their own filth, because they are confident that they can perform their duty toward him by ridiculous acts of expiation. Then while their trust ought to have been placed in him, they neglect him and rely upon themselves, his creatures though they be. Finally, they entangle themselves in such a huge mass of errors that blind wickedness stifles and finally extinguishes those sparks which once flashed forth to show them God's glory. Yet that seed remains which can in no wise be uprooted: that there is some sort of divinity; but this seed is so corrupted by itself it produces only the worst fruits.[36]

Thus, the phenomenon of hypocrisy is actually a confirmation of a key doctrine in biblical anthropology.

CONCLUSION

Hypocrisy is a multifaceted vice which can be condemned on a number of counts. Each of the three major moral traditions considers hypocritical behavior to be wrong but for different reasons. From a utilitarian standpoint, hypocrisy is wrong because it kills the moral spirit of the hypocrite himself, undermining the incentive to live morally. Plus, the net social consequences of this vice are probably more negative than positive. Kantian ethics condemns hypocrisy because (1) it is necessarily performed with bad intentions, (2) it cannot be universalized, and (3) it is disrespectful of persons, necessarily treating them solely as means rather than also as ends in themselves. Finally, the virtue ethicist would reject hypocrisy as a vice that opposes some virtues essential to the good life, such as honesty, justice, conscientiousness, integrity, and civic-mindedness.

At Least I'm Not a Hypocrite

The Apologetic Problem of Hypocrisy

When the fox preaches, look to your geese.
German Proverb

It is no fault of Christianity that a hypocrite falls into sin.
St. Jerome

If it is surprising that Christian scholars have not explored the subject of hypocrisy in much depth, it is all the more surprising that apologists have rarely addressed the skeptical objection from hypocrisy. Critics of the faith often cite Christians' hypocrisies, ranging from the Spanish Inquisition to the escapades of some contemporary televangelists. Instances of gross hypocrisy provide ammunition for skeptics who complain that Christianity cannot be an adequate answer to the problems facing humankind if its practitioners prove no better morally than unbelievers whose needs they aim to address. How can the Christians' truth claims be taken seriously, the skeptic asks, when glaring inconsistencies exist in their own house? Why listen to the Christian message of redemption when it is so often accompanied by sham righteousness? In short, the skeptic says, Christians are not really better than anyone else, so don't listen to them.

In this chapter I will identify and distinguish a range of skeptical postures toward the claim that Christianity is exclusively true, drawing from three scholars who base their views, at least in part, upon the observation that practicing Christians are not morally superior to other persons. I will also pose several versions of the apologetic problem of hypocrisy, ultimately arriving at what I conceive to be the most challenging formulation of the objection. Finally, I will identify some possible explanations as to why Christian theism is especially prone to the objection from hypocrisy.

SKEPTICISM, RELIGIOUS PLURALISM, AND CHRISTIAN EXCLUSIVISM

Skepticism is probably as old as philosophy itself and has taken many forms, but the fundamental characteristic of all skeptics is the attitude of doubt. Some epistemologists distinguish between global and local skepticism. The global skeptic suspends judgment on all truth claims, maintaining that we cannot know anything at all. Such thoroughgoing doubters are rare, but they do exist.[1] The local skeptic, on the other hand, suspends judgment regarding some issue or other. Such a person may dogmatize on many subjects, but when it comes to a particular question, say, the moral permissibility of capital punishment, the aesthetic merit of the Beatles' "White Album," or the existence of extraterrestrial intelligence, she is noncommittal. Probably all of us fall into this category on some issue, which is why the term skeptic as a philosophical label is usually reserved for global skeptics.

Those who affirm the truth of a particular viewpoint to the exclusion of all other points of view on a subject are called exclusivists. A person who maintains that the death penalty is immoral, that the "White Album" is aesthetically excellent, and that intelligent aliens do exist is an exclusivist on each of these issues. And a person who maintains that his or her religious perspective is the correct one is likewise an exclusivist.[2] Traditionally, orthodox Christians have tended to be religious exclusivists (believing that salvation comes only through Jesus Christ), though in recent years this matter has been the subject of much debate among Christian philosophers.[3]

In light of the preceding distinctions, we may identify three broad categories of skeptical attitudes toward the historic Christian exclusivist position, distinguished according to the scope of one's doubt about the possibility of knowledge. First, there is global skepticism, which, as noted above, is constituted by doubt about the possibility of knowledge generally.[4] Second, there is religious skepticism, which rejects all claims to knowledge of religious truth specifically, but which is not necessarily skeptical about the possibility of knowledge in other subjects. Third, there is religious pluralism. This view affirms the possibility of knowledge of religious truth but rejects religious exclusivism.[5] The pluralist claims that not one but a plurality of religious perspectives are actually correct.

Among the tactics used by skeptics to rebuff religious exclusivism is the appeal to the inconsistency of believers' conduct and convictions. Specifically, some philosophers have critiqued religious perspectives on the practical grounds that their doctrines, however logically compelling, do not positively affect the lives of believers. And religious truth, the argument goes, must make a practical moral difference. Three examples of such an approach follow, to be found in the works of John Hick, David Hume, and Bertrand Russell.

Hick's Religious Pluralism

The most renowned contemporary religious pluralist is John Hick. His personal as well as scholarly journey traces the gradual move from a strong Christian exclusivism (of a particularly rigid fundamentalist bent) to his current religious pluralism, which embraces many religious points of view as equally true and accurate expressions of a deeper, essentially mysterious, spiritual reality.[6] In addition to appealing to what he conceives as a common "core" moral teaching among the major world religions (i.e., Christianity, Judaism, Islam, Hinduism, Buddhism), Hick also addresses the matter of moral conduct among sages and other devotees in each of these religions. What he sees is not the moral superiority of Christians, nor of any other religious group, but moral parity among devout practitioners within these traditions. Beginning with the concept of a saint as "a person who is much further advanced than most of us in the transformation from self-centeredness to Reality-centeredness," he argues that "each of the great religious traditions seems, so far as we can tell, to promote this transformation in one form or another to about the same extent. Relating this to the traditional assumption of superiority, I am thus suggesting that we have no good grounds for maintaining that Christianity has produced or is producing more saints, in proportion to population, or a higher quality of saintliness, than any other of the great streams of religious life."[7]

This is to say that the Christian religion can boast neither a quantitative nor qualitative evidential advantage over other world religions when it comes to its inspiration of positive moral conduct. Of course, Hick admits the difficulty (perhaps, even, impossibility) of such an assessment, as it relies upon "partial and unsystematic" evidence. Nevertheless, he believes he has grounds to maintain that "we are not in a position to assert a greater power in Christianity than in any of the other great world faiths to bring about the kind of transformation in human beings that we all desire."[8]

In addition to this parity argument from positive moral effects of world religions, Hick uses a parallel argument focusing on the alleged negative moral effects of Christianity to undermine its claim to exclusive truth: "Christianity, though providing in recent centuries a birthplace for modern science and a home for the modern liberal ideals of equality and freedom, has generated savage wars of religion and supported innumerable 'just wars'; has tortured and burned multitudes of heretics and witches in the name of God; has motivated and authorized the persecution of the Jews; has validated systematic racism; and has tolerated the Western capitalist 'rape of the earth,' the misuse of nuclear energy, and the basic injustice of the North-South division into rich and poor nations."[9]

Hick's argument is double-pronged, emphasizing that Christianity is no more effective in producing moral saints or quelling moral vice than other religions. The net result, to Hick's mind, is that there are no practical grounds, in terms of moral conduct, to regard Christianity as the one true religion. He concludes that "the world traditions seem to be more or less on a par with each other. None can be singled out as manifestly superior."[10]

While, as we shall see below, there is an important point at the heart of Hick's objection to Christian exclusivism, there is a critical flaw in his construction of each of these arguments. First, the positive parity argument depends crucially on the assumption that Christianity does not produce more or greater saints than other religions (relative to their respective populations). But can Hick reasonably claim to know this? This is a premise that needs empirical support. But such evidence neither he nor anyone else can produce, for it is too general a claim. How would one go about making a systematic and (sufficiently) comprehensive review of all the saints of the world religions to make even a remotely trustworthy comparison? Given the limits of empirical inquiry, such a test is impossible. But this daunting prospect does not keep Hick from casually asserting his premise.[11] He simply assumes what he could not possibly know. Hick's reasoning is no less brazen in his negative-effects parity argument. Note that in declaring that Christianity "has generated wars," "burned multitudes," "motivated and authorized the persecution of the Jews," "validated systematic racism," and so forth, he recklessly glosses over the controversial and substantive question as to the precise cause of these heinous deeds. Is it *Christianity* or misinformed *Christians* that are really to blame? Hick seems blind to this simple but profoundly important distinction.

Hume's Pyrrhonistic Skepticism

David Hume is well known for his skeptical arguments aimed at undermining religious belief. His critiques of the theistic argument from design and belief in miracles are still widely discussed today. In the concluding section of his *Dialogues Concerning Natural Religion,* Hume presents an argument against "popular religion" (presumably Christianity) based on some of the same concerns raised by Hick. But Hume's arguments have significantly more bite. His thesis seems to be that belief in the Christian religion is no better than rejection of religion altogether when it comes to inspiring moral conduct. That is, in the practical sphere a thoroughgoing naturalism is as valid as Christian belief.

Speaking through Philo, his primary mouthpiece in the dialogue,[12] Hume begins by noting that "[t]he proper office of religion is to regulate the heart of men, humanize their conduct, infuse the spirit of temperance, order, and obedience."[13] But contrary to its manifest purpose, religion is more likely to be unfavorable to morality. Hume has three main reasons for making this claim. First, whereas one's natural inclinations have a steady effect upon one's behavior, "religious motives, where they act at all, operate only by starts and bounds; and it is scarcely possible for them to become altogether habitual to the mind."[14] Second, the preoccupation with personal salvation tends to "extinguish the benevolent affections, and beget a narrow, contracted selfishness."[15] And third, the terrors inspired by religion (the fear of judgment and damnation) preoccupy believers, causing them to brood and despair and distract them from a proper attention to right living. The net result of these sorts of psychological dynamics operant within believers, according to Hume, is that "many religious exercises are entered into with seeming fervour, where the heart, at the time, feels cold and languid: A habit of dissimulation is by degrees contracted: And fraud and falsehood become the predominant principle. Hence the reason of that vulgar observation, that the highest zeal in religion and the deepest hypocrisy, so far from being inconsistent, are often or commonly united in the same individual character."[16]

Apparently Hume's point is that religious belief, at least of a traditionally theistic sort, causes rather than cures hypocrisy. This is a strong claim, potentially devastating for the religious apologist. But he goes even further, asserting that where the religiously devout are allowed freedom of expression, one can expect "nothing but endless disputes, quarrels, factions, persecutions, and civil commotions."[17] And since "true religion has no such pernicious consequences," we can conclude that the popular religion (i.e., Christianity), for all its appeal to the masses, is not true.[18]

What are we to make of this argument? Of course, granting the truth of Hume's premises, the Christian's best response is simply to deny that her faith commitment is properly represented by its "popular" expression. This line of response is given by Cleanthes in the dialogue, who warns Philo: "Allow not your zeal against false religion to undermine your veneration of the true."[19] This remark is quite to the point. But it is easy to see just why Hume's mistake is made by those who use this sort of argument. For one thing, the suffering caused in the name of religion in nearly every epoch of recorded history is exasperating. And it is a natural, if rash, human response to want to purge society of any elements which are so constantly associated with strife and injustice. But this would be irresponsible for several reasons. First, as was noted in the previous discussion of Hick, sorting out causes and effects in this matter is a very tricky task. It is difficult to determine in any particular case whether a person's actions are prompted by her religion's actual teachings or due to an improper interpretation or warped expression of sound doctrine. Such questions become that much more complex and difficult to address when it comes to society-wide conflicts. Second, in terms of religious psychology, a pivotal issue needs to be teased out, namely that concerning the difference between the mature, healthy-minded believer and the immature or psychologically handicapped believer. No religion should be blamed for the misdeeds of its emotionally sick adherents. Finally, the problem of inductive support for a key premise plagues Hume's argument every bit as much as it does Hick's. How do we know that the sort of psychological dynamic leading to hypocrisy, as described by Hume, is actually more common in religious devotees than in nonbelievers? Hume, again like Hick, relies upon intuition and speculation rather than argument or empirical evidence to justify this bold claim. Indeed, their common error might just result from the fact that such evidence cannot be produced.

Russell's Religious Skepticism

In his famous essay "Why I Am Not a Christian," Bertrand Russell critiques the Christian worldview on a number of fronts. One of his objections pertains to hypocrisy, as he notes that although Jesus taught, for example, that we must give to all who ask and not turn away from those who want to borrow, Christians do not put such principles into practice. Russell writes, "there is one other maxim of Christ which I think has a great deal in it, but I do not find that it is very popular among some of our Christian friends. He says, 'If thou wilt be perfect, go and sell that which thou hast, and give to the poor.' That is a very excellent maxim, but, as I say, it is not much practiced. All these, I think, are good maxims, although they are a little difficult to live up to. I do not profess to live up to them myself; but then, after all, it is not quite the same thing as for a Christian."[20]

Christians, then, do not practice what their Lord preached. So according to Russell, this constitutes a mark against their worldview. Or at least these are grounds for his rejecting the Christian faith. It is interesting to note that Russell here admits that these are "good maxims" taught by Jesus, and this is a compliment to the moral teachings of Christ. This means that, as far as this objection goes, Russell objects neither to the content of Christian teaching nor to Jesus himself. So it must be the present-day followers of Jesus with whom he takes issue—not for their foolishness in following Christ but for their failure to follow him well. Ironically, then, Russell's criticism amounts to just the same sort of exhortation to Christians which they sometimes give one another—to live up to the teachings of their master.

Russell recognizes that the difficulty of fulfilling a moral ideal, for all the trouble and inconsistency it may produce, does not impugn the moral ideal itself. But he does not seem to realize that one's likely failure to live up to a high ideal is not sufficient grounds for rejecting it. In many contexts, moral and otherwise, those persons who expect more of themselves, achieve more. It has been said (by Goethe, I think) that one must sometimes overestimate his abilities in order to realize his potential. If this is the case, then maintaining the highest of moral ideals might be of some assistance in striving to live the good life.

Although it is not relevant to this present study, Russell does go on to criticize the moral character of Christ himself (because of such actions as fatally casting demons into a herd of swine and his teachings about hell). Such an assessment of the founder of the Christian faith is probably more to the point when it comes to the moral evaluation of Christianity than focusing on the moral faults of its adherents. But since most religious skeptics acknowledge the moral goodness of Christ (even Russell demotes him only below Socrates and Buddha), he is rarely the target of moral criticism.

Even if these arguments of Hick, Hume, and Russell are sound, they do not by themselves show that Christian exclusivism is false. This is because to deny practical moral grounds for preferring a particular religious viewpoint is not to deny all evidentiary grounds for doing so. Even if successful, such arguments only disqualify one category of potential evidence, however significant, for the truth of a religious point of view. The pivotal question which remains to be asked, from the standpoint of Christian apologetics, is whether there is additional evidential support for the exclusivist claim. For instance, is there sufficient warrant for believing the Old and New Testament documents to be divinely inspired and, therefore, finally authoritative? Specifically, is there external evidence for divine inspiration to be gleaned from philological, archaeological, scientific, and historical inquiry? And is there internal evidence for divine inspiration to be found in the Old and New Testaments in the form of fulfilled predictive prophecy or profound doctrinal consistency (across diverse cultures and many centuries)? Or taking a different tack, one may ask whether there is some other warrant for believing in the exclusive truth of Christian theism, whether that takes the form of religious experience, claims of miraculous divine intervention, or some other special divine disclosure.[21] These questions have enormous range, sweeping across numerous academic disciplines. It is therefore with the utmost humility and caution that skeptics, pluralists, and exclusivists should make their claims about religious truth.

FORMALIZING THE PROBLEM OF HYPOCRISY

We have seen how the skeptical objections from hypocrisy offered by Hick, Hume, and Russell are spoiled by, among other things, a fatal reliance upon intuition and general impressions in assessing the practical merits of the Christian religion. In spite of their failures, I believe the objection from hypocrisy can be sharpened considerably, as I shall attempt to demonstrate. But to avoid the pitfalls of the above arguments, the skeptic's target must be internal to the Christian worldview, ultimately pertaining to one of its essential teachings. Focus upon the interface of doctrine and practice will never advance the religious skeptic's case until some central theological doctrine is plainly shown to be falsified by believers' hypocrisy. Furthermore, a successful version of the objection from hypocrisy cannot critically depend upon questionable general claims but must assume only obviously true premises about the immorality of devout Christians. For starters, consider this formulation of the problem:

Version 1

1. An essential teaching of Christian theism is that Christians gain moral redemption through faith in Jesus Christ.
2. Some Christians act immorally.
3. To act immorally demonstrates that one is not morally redeemed.
4. Therefore, Christianity is essentially false.

Now this argument is formally valid. But is it sound? The first premise seems to be true, as one of the central themes of the Bible is that there is moral redemption for the recipients of God's grace. And the second premise is obvious. (Note that it does not depend upon questionable generalizations based upon casual impressions from personal experience or history.) It is the third premise which is problematic. The reason is that it implies a flawed conception of moral redemption. Specifically, it assumes a perfectionist view of sanctification which Christians reject, as was noted in chapter 5, because it is biblically indefensible. The view most at home with the Scriptures recognizes that moral redemption implies not moral perfection but (1) moral justification, involving the forgiveness of one's sins (original and actually performed), (2) moral repentance, which involves a resolve to live a life morally pleasing to God, and (3) a process of moral improvement or sanctification, whereby the redeemed person steadily advances in her quest for obedience to God's moral law. Notice that none of these three elements of moral redemption are inconsistent with occasional immoral acts.

On top of this, the third premise is counterintuitive. It defies common sense to suggest that moral redemption implies the attainment of absolute moral perfection. This is why such phrases as "nobody's perfect" and "to err is human" are cliches. They point to basic facts about the human condition that any sound philosophical anthropology or moral theory must acknowledge, however strong its insistence upon the reality of moral redemption.

All of this shows the absurdity of premise three in the argument, which is to say that the argument as a whole is unsound. But, it may be added, even if perfectionism were true, it would not imply that the argument is sound, for one could simply say that anyone who sins has yet to be morally perfected (since on such a view, presumably, moral perfection would be attained gradually, not instantaneously). This is certainly not the route I would take. It is, however, one more way of showing this version of the argument to be unsound.

In light of these points, the skeptic might reformulate the objection from hypocrisy by focusing on the key manifestation of moral redemption, namely moral improvement. For if the Christian doctrine of redemption is to have any relevant practical application, there must be some means of evaluating this worldview in the crucible of believers' conduct. Consider version 2, a revision of the argument:

Version 2

1. An essential teaching of Christian theism is that Christians gain moral redemption through faith in Jesus Christ which is manifested in moral improvement.
2. Some Christians are guilty of gross moral misconduct.
3. To commit gross moral misconduct is to prove that one is not morally improving.
4. Therefore, Christianity is essentially false.

This version of the problem could use some clarification, specifically regarding the phrase "moral improvement." First, "moral improvement" should be understood as a necessary but not a sufficient condition for moral redemption. That is, it is implied by but does not itself imply moral redemption. Second, we may understand this phrase as denoting at least an increase of success in adhering to the moral law.

So what of the status of this argument? The first two premises do seem to be true. However, the third premise, though plausible at first blush, is false. For this proposition ignores the fact that "moral improvement" is a relative notion. This is so in two respects. First, moral improvement is relative to a moral career. While to commit a sin in any case can be seen as a moral regression relative to the agent's obedience immediately preceding the act, if we adjust our perspective, looking at the person's life over, say, a two or three month span, we may see the act as an aberration in a period of her life which on the whole represents genuine moral improvement.

Second, moral improvement is also to a significant degree relative to a person's natural constitution. In short, people are gifted with differing degrees of psychological raw material with which to work in their quest for the morally good life. C. S. Lewis makes this observation:

> When a man who has been perverted from his youth and taught that cruelty is the right thing, does some tiny little kindness, or refrains from some cruelty he might have committed, and thereby, perhaps, risks being sneered at by his companions, he may, in God's eyes, be doing more than you and I would do if we gave up life itself for a friend.

It is as well to put this the other way round. Some of us who seem quite nice people may, in fact, have made so little use of a good heredity and a good upbringing that we are really worse than those whom we regard as fiends. Can we be quite sure how we should have behaved if we had been saddled with the psychological outfit, and then with the bad upbringing, and then with the power, say, of Himmler? That is why Christians are told not to judge.[22]

If Lewis is right, then in declaring on the basis of a particular vice that a person has not morally improved we run the risk of committing the fallacy of "hypothesis contrary to fact." For in the case of the redeemed sinner we have no sufficiently clear idea as to how the person would have acted had she never converted to Christianity. To make this judgment is to pretend to have access to data that one simply does not have.

I do not mean to suggest that Christianity is entirely untestable as a hypothesis about the human condition and the cure for what morally ails us. But I don't believe it to be testable on a person by person basis, for when it comes to individuals, we lack in any particular case a "control" with which to compare the redeemed person. Our only epistemological recourse, then, in testing the Christian redemption hypothesis from the practical standpoint of moral improvement might lie in analysis of the overall population, in asking questions such as, Are Christians on the whole more or less likely to act piously than non-Christians? As was noted earlier, this question is not susceptible to definitive empirical testing, but if one were to proceed in a rational inquiry about the evidential significance of hypocrisy in the church, then something along these lines would be the necessary approach.

Does this rendering of the Christian doctrine of moral improvement trivialize the concept of moral redemption? For we can never confidently say that a particular person is indeed morally redeemed, because we cannot be certain if she is demonstrating moral improvement (since we do not know how she would have acted had she not become a Christian). First, this is an epistemological problem, but not for the Christian exclusively. It is a problem for anyone who believes in moral redemption, regardless of her moral tradition—utilitarian, Kantian, Islamic, Jewish, and so forth. And anything that argues against all moral traditions argues against none in particular. Second, the prospects for assessing a person's moral growth or regression, though troubled, are far from hopeless. A prerequisite for success, however, as I have suggested, is that we adopt the larger "macro" perspective on the individual's moral career rather than succumb to the temptation to be blinded by a person's most recent behavior. A particularly heinous sin may prove to be an exception to the rule in an otherwise consistently obedient life.

But what of the even more challenging cases when Christians' acts of serious moral impropriety are not occasional but habitual? Or instances in which the person's grave sins represent moral regression even relative to her moral career, such as when a devout believer becomes involved in an adulterous relationship and continues in it unrepentant. In light of such examples, the following revision of the argument from hypocrisy can be made:

Version 3

1. An essential teaching of Christianity is that Christians gain moral redemption through faith in Jesus Christ which is manifested in moral improvement.
2. Some Christians display moral regression by performing acts of gross moral misconduct on a regular basis.
3. Anyone who morally regresses is not morally improving.
4. Therefore, Christianity is essentially false.

This formulation of the argument from hypocrisy seems to me the strongest available to the skeptic. And it is to this version of the problem that I have the least original response. I admit that cases of habitual egregious sin committed by believers are as theologically and philosophically mystifying as they are personally heartrending. But the Christian does have practical guidelines as to how to make assessments in such instances. The biblical litmus test is well known. Jesus tells us that we can judge a tree by its fruits.[23] John says that anyone who continues in willful sin cannot be "born of God."[24] And

James says a faith is known by the works that it inspires.[25] When it comes to the unrepentant adulterer, for example, who claims to be a believer in Christ, it is just such a person whose moral redemption, from a biblical standpoint, we must doubt. Of course, in some particular cases it is very difficult, perhaps impossible, to tell if a person is redeemed when applying this test. But as Aristotle says, we should not expect more precision from the science of moral inquiry than the subject matter allows. It is sometimes a messy business.

This last formulation of the problem is very instructive. For it is precisely when the skeptic's objection from hypocrisy seems most strong that the Christian properly resorts to her own skepticism, specifically regarding the claim of moral redemption made by one who is morally regressing. On this score Christians could perhaps afford to be even stronger in their stance. This certainly seems to be the case if John's words in 1 John 3 and the apostle Paul's model for excommunication in 1 Corinthians 5 are to be taken seriously. Could the salient lesson for us Christians be that we have a mandate to be stricter church disciplinarians? One wonders if the prevalence of hypocrisy in the church would be comparable to what it is now if we were much more adamant in calling one another to account for our actions.

Here is a final version of the problem of hypocrisy, which pivots upon the dimension of intentional deception involved in some instances of this vice:

Version 4

1. If Christians are morally redeemed through their faith in Christ, then they should be more likely than most to be forthright about their moral condition.
2. Christians are not more likely than most to be forthright about their moral condition (in fact, they are more likely than most to deceive others about their true piety).
3. Therefore, Christians are not really morally redeemed through their faith in Christ.

The first premise, it would seem, is supported by the general thesis held by Christians that moral redemption through

Christ is likely to make a person more honest and sincere. The second premise constitutes an empirical claim. In evaluating this argument we may, for starters, question the truth of the first premise. To do so might seem to be antithetical to the Christian moral ideals of honesty and sincerity. However, when we take into account the complexity of some situations and how often a person experiences the tension created by the endeavor to fulfill sometimes conflicting ideals, we see that sometimes such deception can have a laudable motive. It is ironic, in fact, that it may sometimes reveal a feature of the Christian's psychology that is in a sense flattering to our worldview. For the intentional deception of others regarding one's true piety is sometimes symptomatic of two positive characteristics: (1) shame for one's sin, and (2) a desire to avoid disappointing others or being a stumbling block to their faith. Of course, when someone is involved in self-deception it becomes a different matter entirely, hardly to be commended. But I doubt that anyone would seriously defend a version of the objection from hypocrisy based solely on self-deception, mainly because it is one of the prerequisites of being a Christian that one acknowledge and confess one's sin and need for forgiveness.

As is now evident, I believe the first premise of this argument itself to be questionable, but I think the more promising strategy is to attack the second premise. We have already seen from our analyses of preceding arguments how generalizations such as these need to be supported by empirical evidence. Those who use such arguments, and I have encountered many, tend to be anecdotal in their evidential support for the claim in premise two. But anecdotal evidence will not suffice. So the skeptic again seems to be stuck.

WHY CHRISTIANS ARE PRONE TO THE ACCUSATION OF HYPOCRISY

If the skeptical objection from hypocrisy so plainly fails to undermine Christian belief, why is it so popular? If it is not because there is a flaw in the Christian worldview, what is the explanation? I think there are a number of reasons why Christian theism is often the target of this objection.

First, it is difficult to live the Christian life. The moral ideal of Christianity is nothing less than perfection. Jesus himself commanded that his followers be perfect as God is perfect. There is no higher standard, and this is one that is, of course, impossible to live up to. But as noted earlier, the difficulty of attaining ultimate success in living by one's moral ideal is not a good reason for relinquishing it.

Second, Christians are sinners. Conversion does not change this fundamental fact about human nature (though it should result in a change of the general outlook and moral trajectory of one's life). In fact, as a hypothesis about the moral condition of human beings, Christian theism would actually predict a certain amount of hypocrisy on the part of its converts.[26] As was noted in chapter 5, the Christian affirms the reality of original sin in all human beings, a powerful innate tendency to violate the moral law of God. However, not all sins are sins of hypocrisy, a fact sometimes overlooked by critics of Christianity. When this distinction is overlooked, it is to be expected that accusations of hypocrisy will fly, unfounded though they be.

Third, Christianity's doctrine of salvation is based on divine grace rather than human merit. This is perhaps one reason for what I regard as the illusion of the prevalence of Christian hypocrites. It is, after all, easier to masquerade as a Christian than, say, a devout Muslim, orthodox Jew, or Theravadan Buddhist. This owes to the fact that although Christianity, like any other religion, has its rituals, its visible spiritual disciplines tend to be less rigorous and demanding than those of many other religions. It demands no extreme asceticism, public prayers, nor forsaking of one's possessions. Consequently, a non-Christian can "play along," for any number of reasons, without being overly burdened by the demands of his artificial faith. Then when he gives in to grievous sin, the illusion of Christian hypocrisy is fostered.

Thus there are good reasons to expect that the Christian church will be accused of hypocrisy. They owe principally to the combination of these key features of Christian theism: (1) it is a religion whose standard of conduct is divine perfection, a practically unattainable goal for mere mortals, (2) its assessment of the moral condition of human beings is complex, though not incoherent, emphasizing the innate sinful human nature, the manifestations of which are not fully obliterated, even after salvation, and (3) it is a religion which teaches salvation by grace, not human merit, thus making masquerading easier to perform and harder to detect.

SOME FURTHER OBSERVATIONS

A few other points are relevant to the Christian's response to the objection from hypocrisy. First, we must not confuse the sins of non-Christians in the church with Christians' hypocrisy. Since the Christian church welcomes sinners, there will always be unrepentant persons in its midst, not as members, hopefully, but as inquirers, though some may be careless pagans or deliberate impostors. Undoubtedly, the sins of such persons are sometimes construed as the sins of Christians, in which case the church is blamed for the guilt of outsiders.

Second, when sincere Christians do in fact sin grievously on occasion, the term hypocrisy is sometimes misapplied. Often—perhaps even most of the time—Christians sin not because they are self-conscious deceivers but because they are overcome by temptation. They suffer from moral weakness. As we saw in chapters 4 and 5, a biblical view recognizes the struggle with sin to be a difficult one in which the believer is likely to frequently fail. In this sense, Peter's denial of Christ is a paradigm case, with which any Christian can readily identify. He said one thing (i.e., vowed he would never forsake Jesus) and did another (i.e., denied him three times). However, he is not properly dubbed a hypocrite, for he was quite morally serious and was not self-deceived about the morality of his act of denial. He simply gave in to temptation under duress. His was a sin, to be sure, but it was not the sin of hypocrisy. I believe the overwhelming majority of sins committed by Christians fall into this category of moral weakness.

Third, the problem of hypocrisy in the church is in one sense a compliment to biblical morality. Why would anyone want to make a charade of being a Christian if this were not an objectively admirable thing? If hypocrisy really is the tribute that vice pays to virtue, then those who make a pretense of being Christians inadvertently pay homage to our worldview. It is a backhanded compliment to the high moral standards of the Christian faith. As Bertrand Russell says, Jesus offers us "*good* maxims."

Finally, objections from hypocrisy really miss their mark if one is attempting to attack the Christian faith at its heart. To do this, one has a much harder task than merely proving that Christ's followers are sometimes hypocritical. Rather, one must show that Jesus himself was a hypocrite. To succeed in proving this is an incomparably difficult task, since he is almost unanimously regarded not only as morally decent but as morally exceptional. Undoubtedly, it is precisely for this reason that such attempts are not forthcoming.

CONCLUSION

This analysis demonstrates that the objection from hypocrisy can be adequately answered by the Christian. In fact, each version of the problem discussed can be challenged on several counts. I would add this tactical point for the apologist: the problem of hypocrites in the church is a valuable point of contact for relating to skeptics who raise this objection. Jesus himself spent a great deal of time exposing the duplicity of religious leaders of his day. His most stern rebukes, in fact, were directed toward such persons. It can be helpful to remind skeptics that they already share something in common with Jesus: a hatred of hypocrisy.

Conclusion

Conviction is worthless unless it is converted into conduct.
Thomas Carlyle

Let unswerving integrity ever be your watchword.
Bernard Baruch

Hypocrisy is a complex phenomenon with a variety of manifestations, but it essentially involves an inconsistency between one's actions and what one believes, says, or does. There are two roots of hypocrisy: self-deception and a lack of moral seriousness. In the former case, hypocrisy is a first-order moral vice, while in the latter it is a second-order vice (or metavice). The person who lacks moral seriousness only pretends to respect the moral law, while the self-deceived hypocrite genuinely believes she is acting morally, when in fact she is not.

Determining the nature of self-deception is a tricky matter. The phenomenon is paradoxical, for the self-deceived person seems to deny what she knows to be true. Among the models discussed, I proposed a hybrid account which identifies two species of self-deception. One form of self-deceit arises at the cognitive level, where a person develops a false belief as a result of a motivated bias. The other kind is volitional in nature, involving a disavowal of one's behavior. Either form of self-deception can give rise to hypocrisy.

145

Moral weakness, or *akrasia,* is related to hypocrisy but essentially distinct from it. The key difference between these two forms of moral failing is that the morally weak person genuinely regrets her failure, while the hypocrite does not, either because she is self-deceived and does not believe she has sinned or because she is not morally serious. Like self-deception, the notion of moral weakness suggests a paradox. How can a person sincerely believe that a particular action is best and yet fail to do it, when she is free to perform that act? Siding with the Aristotelian approach to *akrasia,* as opposed to the Socratic approach, I defended the view that the morally weak person acts against her better judgment as a result of the overwhelming influence of some noncognitive forces of the mind.

In spite of the innate human tendency toward sin, we have reason to be hopeful in our moral struggle. First, moral justification before God is available to us through the atoning work of Christ. Second, sanctification or moral improvement is possible and expected in the life of the Christian. In this process, deliberate self-training to improve one's capacity for self-control is appropriate. I outlined a variety of theological conceptions of sanctification and noted that none of these endorses the view that a Christian can attain moral perfection in this life.

Hypocrisy can be assessed from the perspective of three different moral points of view: utilitarianism, Kantian ethics, and virtue ethics. The utilitarian condemns hypocrisy because of its negative impact on the hypocritical individual as well as society in general. The Kantian rejects hypocrisy as immoral because, among other reasons, it is disrespectful of persons. And the virtue ethicist regards hypocrisy as immoral because it directly contradicts the life of virtue in which such traits as honesty, justice, and integrity are displayed. Hypocrisy, then, is condemned across the major moral traditions, though for a variety of reasons. This explains why it is especially despised among the vices: it is wrong at so many levels.

Lastly, the apologetic problem of hypocrisy is a real and important one for defenders of the Christian faith. However, the presence of hypocrites in the church does not undermine the main claims of the Christian faith. On the contrary, the problem of hypocrisy actually confirms the basic Christian teaching about the fallenness of human nature. Furthermore, given the biblical doctrine of salvation by grace through faith, it is to be expected that moral frauds will be more prevalent in the Christian church than in other religious traditions. Therefore, serious critics of Christianity would be better advised to focus their moral complaints on Jesus himself, who alone is claimed by Christians to be without sin. This is not to say that the behavior of Christians is not apologetically relevant. It is rather to emphasize that the failure of particular Christians does not imply the falsity of their worldview.

This inquiry into moral fraud and its related vices has led us down many difficult paths. Perhaps such difficulties explain why so few Christian scholars have assumed the burden of addressing these issues and why this book is, regrettably, the first of its kind. This work does not constitute a definitive Christian statement on hypocrisy and the other vices discussed. But I hope it will inspire further research into and discussion of these issues and be of service to others who wish to do similar work.

An assessment of whether the particular conceptions of hypocrisy, self-deception, and moral weakness defended here are at least approximately correct must await the responses of my peers. What cannot wait, however, is our own personal commitment to avoid these vices. Toward that end, the Christian's mandate is as straightforward as it is a profound moral challenge: be morally serious; be self-controlled; and avoid self-deception.

Notes

Chapter 1: The Mother of All Vices

1. *Tartuffe,* act 1, scene 5. Quoted from *The Misanthrope and Tartuffe,* trans. Richard Wilbur (New York: Harcourt, Brace, and World, Inc., 1954), 187–88.

2. Ibid., act 4, scene 5, 288.

3. 1 Sam. 28:5–10.

4. David's judgment demanding the man pay fourfold for his sin is in keeping with Old Testament law. As a colleague of mine has suggested, it is perhaps not coincidental that David would eventually lose four of his sons in tragic circumstances: the son borne by Bathsheba (died in infancy), Amnon (killed by Absalom's men), Absalom (killed by David's men), and Adonijah (killed by Solomon's men).

5. 2 Sam. 12:1–7.

6. Matt. 26:33–35, 69–75.

7. Plato, *Republic,* bk. 2, trans. Paul Shorey, in *The Collected Dialogues of Plato,* eds. Edith Hamilton and Huntington Cairns (New Jersey: Princeton University Press, 1961), 608.

8. Thomas Aquinas, *Summa Theologica,* trans. English Dominican Fathers (New York: Benziger Brothers, Inc., 1947), vol. 2 (2.2.111.1), 1669.

9. Ibid., 1670.

10. G. W. F. Hegel, *Philosophy of Right,* trans. T. M. Knox (Oxford: Oxford University Press, 1952), 94.

11. Ibid., 95.

12. G. W. F. Hegel, *Phenomenology of Spirit,* trans. A. V. Miller (Oxford: Oxford University Press, 1977), 401.

13. Joseph Butler, "Upon Self-Deceit," in *Fifteen Sermons* (London: G. Bell and Sons, Ltd., 1964), 151.

14. Ibid., 153.

15. Ibid., 153–54.

16. Ibid., 158.

17. Jean Paul Sartre, *Being and Nothingness,* trans. Hazel E. Barnes (New York: Washington Square Press, 1956), 89.

18. Ibid., 90.

19. Gilbert Ryle, *The Concept of Mind* (London: Hutchinson and Co., 1949), 173.

20. Ibid., 181.

CHAPTER 2: A LIE TOLD BY OUTWARD DEEDS

1. Roger Crisp and Christopher Cowton, "Hypocrisy and Moral Seriousness," *American Philosophical Quarterly* 31, no. 4 (October 1994): 343.

2. Matt. 6:5–6.

3. Crisp and Cowton cite as an example the Pharisees' effort to trap Jesus when questioning him about paying taxes (Matthew 22:15–22).

4. As Crisp and Cowton note, "I may pretend to others that I have some virtue not in order to gain anything from them, but merely because I am too ashamed to admit my fault" ("Hypocrisy and Moral Seriousness," 343).

5. Crisp and Cowton give the following example, which they regard as morally praiseworthy: "Consider an atheist mother who feigns a little piety to the visiting Mother Superior in order to increase her sincerely pious but excessively self-effacing daughter's chances of being accepted into the convent" (ibid.).

6. "Consider, for example, the dissembling teenager who pretends allegiance to the repulsive code of honour of his neighbourhood gang in order to gain acceptance. Nor need 'virtue' be understood here in a narrowly moral sense. Any kind of excellence or perceived excellence can be pretended to hypocritically" (ibid., 344).

7. Ibid., 345.

8. Ibid., 344.

9. Matt. 7:4–5.

10. 2 Sam. 12:5–6.

11. Crisp and Cowton, "Hypocrisy and Moral Seriousness," 345.

12. Judith Sklar, *Ordinary Vices* (Cambridge: The Belknap Press, 1984), 62.

13. 1 Sam. 28.

14. Crisp and Cowton, "Hypocrisy and Moral Seriousness," 345.

15. Matt. 23:23–28.

16. Joseph Butler, "Upon Self-Deceit," in *Fifteen Sermons* (London: G. Bell and Sons, Ltd., 1964), 158.

17. Bela Szabados, "Hypocrisy," *Canadian Journal of Philosophy* 9, no. 2, (June 1979): 209.

18. Raphael Demos, "Lying to Oneself," *Journal of Philosophy* 57 (1960): 590–91.

19. Crisp and Cowton, "Hypocrisy and Moral Seriousness," 347.

20. Though, of course, to say that one is "metavirtuous" in this sense, does not imply that one is "virtuous" (i.e., abides by the moral law). It only means that one acknowledges the existence of a moral law and that it applies to oneself.

21. It is precisely this role-playing for personal gain that distinguishes the metavicious hypocrite from the Nietzschean or Dostoevskian amoralist.

22. Christine McKinnon, "Hypocrisy, with a Note on Integrity," *American Philosophical Quarterly* 28, no. 4 (October 1991): 327.

23. Aristotle, *Nicomachean Ethics*, bk. 1, ch. 3, in W. D. Ross, trans., *The Basic Works of Aristotle*, ed. Richard McKeon (New York: Random House, Inc., 1941), 928.

24. See *The Genealogy of Morals* and *Beyond Good and Evil*. Nietzsche's avowed amoralism was dramatically prefigured in Dostoevski's *Crime and Punishment*, as Raskolnikov declared himself beyond the moral law and committed a premeditated murder to demonstrate this.

25. Butler, "Upon Self-Deceit," 153–55.

26. My answer to this objection follows that of Piers Benn, who says "this view is not supported by the phenomenology of weak-willed conduct, and hard to argue for on conceptual grounds alone." ("What is Wrong with Hypocrisy?" *International Journal of Moral and Social Studies* 8, no. 3 [Autumn 1993]: 225).

27. As Piers Benn asks rhetorically, "The *akrates* professes principles which he does not live up to, and the hypocrite does the same: wherein lies the difference?" (ibid., 226.)

28. Ibid. This is a possibility that Socrates, of course, plainly denies, since "to know the good is to do it." Aristotle takes issue with the Socratic position in *Nicomachean Ethics*, bk. 7, ch. 2, arguing that "this view plainly contradicts the observed facts" in cases where the incontinent person is mastered by passion. Aristotle's own explanation seems to be that the *akrates* simply ignores what he knows.

For insightful discussions of *akrasia* in connection with hypocrisy, see Demos, "Lying to Oneself," 593–95; Szabados, "Hypocrisy," 198–200; and Benn, "What Is Wrong with Hypocrisy?" 225–26.

29. Benn, "What Is Wrong with Hypocrisy?" 233.

30. Ibid., 229. It is precisely because of such benefits that Benn cautions against the brash exposure of hypocrisy, since doing so "generally tends to discredit the preaching of the hypocrite; to bring ridicule upon teaching which may be perfectly sound." Thus, he adds, "those who, for reasons of 'honesty,' feel bound to unmask hypocrisy, should ask themselves whether their motive really is respect for the principles betrayed. If it is, then the course most conductive to respect for them, may well be concealment of the hypocrisy" (234).

31. McKinnon, "Hypocrisy," 324. Similarly, Eva Kittay says the ironic figure "pretends to be worse than he is by virtue of a detachment from the prevalent moral values and at the same time reveals to us the falsity of the appearances by which we judge things." In so doing, "he confronts society with its own moral deficiencies" (Eva F. Kittay, "On Hypocrisy," *Metaphilosophy* 13, nos. 3 and 4 [July/October 1982]: 281).

32. Plato, *Apology* 21b, trans. Hugh Tredennick, in *The Collected Dialogues of Plato*, eds. Edith Hamilton and Huntington Cairns (Princeton: Princeton University Press, 1961), 7.

33. The parallels between Socrates and Jesus go far beyond their irony. See my "Socrates: A Messianic Type for the Gentiles" in *Philosophia Christi* (18:2) for a detailed exposition of their similarities.

34. Phil. 2:5–7.

CHAPTER 3: TAKING ONESELF IN

1. The paradox here is aptly put by Aristotle, who asserted that "it is impossible for anyone to believe the same thing to be and not to be" (*Metaphysics,* 1005, b23).

2. This does not include the skeptical position that there really are no genuine cases of self-deception and that the term is a misnomer. For skeptical accounts see Stanley Paluch, "Self-Deception," *Inquiry* 10 (1967): 268–78; M. R. Haight, *A Study of Self-Deception* (Sussex: Harvester Press, 1980); and David Kipp, "On Self-Deception," *Philosophical Quarterly* 30 (1980): 305–17.

3. Jean Paul Sartre, *Being and Nothingness,* trans. Hazel E. Barnes (New York: Washington Square Press, 1956), 89.

4. Ibid., emphasis in original.

5. Ibid., 97, emphasis in original.

6. Raphael Demos, "Lying to Oneself," *Journal of Philosophy* 57 (1960): 588–95.

7. Ibid., 588.

8. Ibid., emphasis in original.

9. Ibid., 593.

10. For a variant of Demos's model, see David Pugmire's "'Strong' Self-Deception," *Inquiry* 12 (1969): 339–61. Like Demos, Pugmire conceives of self-deception as an instance of lying to oneself, but he maintains that it is accomplished not by averting one's attention from an unwelcome belief but from the details of an unwelcome belief.

11. See the "epistemic" and "existential" models below for examples of such theories that reject the interpersonal model approach.

12. Herbert Fingarette, *Self-Deception* (London: Routledge and Kegan Paul, 1969), 15–16.

13. This analysis changed as Freud's thinking matured. In his later years his view was that in such cases the superego knows X, while the ego believes not-X. At any rate, the key point that is preserved throughout his career is that the different parts of the psyche can have differing belief states.

14. Amelie O. Rorty, "Self-Deception, *Akrasia,* and Irrationality," *Social Science Information* 19, no. 6 (1980): 920.

15. Amelie O. Rorty, "Belief and Self-Deception," *Inquiry* 15 (1972): 405. For a compartmentalist theory similar to Rorty's, see John King-Farlow's "Self-Deceivers and Sartrian Seducers," *Analysis* 23 (1963): 131–36. King-Farlow argues that self-deception involves deception of one aspect of the mind by another, where the self is conceived as a "large, loose sort of committee," with "rotating chairmanship." Members can "question, warn, praise and deceive each other" (135).

16. David Pears, *Motivated Irrationality* (Oxford: Oxford University Press, 1984), chap. 5. Theories such as Pears's which divide the self into subagents are sometimes described as "homuncular."

17. Ibid., 69–70.

18. Theories similar to Pears's are defended by D. W. Hamlyn, "Self-Deception," *Proceedings of the Aristotelian Society* 45 (1971): 45–60 and

T. S. Champlin, "Deceit, Deception, and the Self-Deceiver," *Philosophical Investigations* 17, no. 1 (January 1994): 53–58.

19. Rorty denies that self-deception is always directly motivated, whether by a wish, desire, or anything else. See her "User-Friendly Self-Deception," *Philosophy* 69 (1994): 217.

20. This criticism of unconscious awareness, in fact, predates Freud by at least two centuries. John Locke criticized Gottfried Leibniz' doctrine of innate ideas by insisting that there can be no awareness that is not conscious awareness. See Locke's *Essay Concerning Human Understanding,* bk. 1, ch. 2, sec. 5.

21. Mark Johnston, "Self-Deception and the Nature of Mind," in *Perspectives on Self-Deception,* eds. B. P. McLaughlin and A. O. Rorty (Berkeley: University of California Press, 1988), 64.

22. Paluch, "Self-Deception," 268–78.

23. Ibid., 274.

24. John Canfield and Don Gustavson, "Self-Deception," *Analysis* 23 (1962): 32–36.

25. Ibid., 33, emphasis in original.

26. Ibid., 35.

27. Terence Penelhum, "Pleasure and Falsity," *Philosophy of Mind,* ed. Stuart Hampshire (New York: Harper and Row, 1966), 242–66.

28. Ibid., 259.

29. Ibid.

30. F. A. Siegler, "Demos on Lying to Oneself," *Journal of Philosophy* 59 (1962): 469–75.

31. Ibid., 474.

32. For an extended criticism of Siegler's proposal, see Fingarette, *Self-Deception,* 17–21.

33. James Peterman, "Self-Deception and the Problem of Avoidance," *Southern Journal of Philosophy* 21 (1983): 565–73.

34. Descartes, *Principles of Philosophy,* in *The Philosophical Works of Descartes,* eds. E. S. Haldane and G. R. Ross, vol. 1 (Cambridge: University Press, 1968).

35. Peterman, "Self-Deception and the Problem of Avoidance," 570.

36. Alfred Mele, "Real Self-Deception," *Behavioral and Brain Sciences* 20 (1997): 91–102. Mele suggests the following sufficient conditions for self-deception:

1. The belief that P which S acquires is false.

2. S treats data relevant, or at least seemingly relevant, to the truth of P in a motivationally biased way.

3. This biased treatment is a nondeviant cause of S's acquiring the belief that P.

4. The body of data possessed by S at the time provides greater warrant for not-P than for P.

See also Mele's "Self-Deception," *Philosophical Quarterly* 33, no. 133 (1983): 165–77, and "Recent Work on Self-Deception," *American Philosophical Quarterly* 24, no. 1 (January 1987): 1–17.

37. Ibid., 94. Mele distinguishes these factors of motivated or "hot" bias from those factors characterizing unmotivated or "cold" bias. An example of the latter is the "confirmation bias," which refers to the tendency to search for data confirming rather than falsifying an hypothesis that is being tested. Such a bias is not caused by desire but is a natural psychological tendency, independent of personal wishes and proclivities.

38. Another account of self-deception falling into this category is defended by David Jones. See his "Pervasive Self-Deception" in *Southern Journal of Philosophy* 27, no. 2 (1989): 217–37.

39. Newton da Costa and Steven French, "Belief, Contradiction and the Logic of Self-Deception," *American Philosophical Quarterly* 27, no. 3 (July 1990): 182.

40. Mele, "Self-Deception," 373, emphasis in original. Among writers on self-deception who agree with Mele's view is Robert Audi, who asserts that "the sincere avowals of the self-deceiver . . . do not express beliefs. . . . in the attribution of beliefs, actions speak louder than words" ("Self-Deception and Rationality" in *Self-Deception and Self-Understanding,* ed. Mike W. Martin [Lawrence, Kans.: University Press of Kansas, 1985], 173).

41. Johnston, "Self-Deception and the Nature of Mind," 67.

42. Steven Hales, "Self-Deception and Belief Attribution," *Synthese* 101 (1994): 283–84.

43. I borrow this example from Amelie O. Rorty in "The Deceptive Self: Liars, Layers, and Lairs," *Perspectives on Self-Deception,* eds. Brian P. McLaughlin and Amelie O. Rorty (Berkeley: University of California Press, 1988), 11. Hales uses this example as a paradigm case in his "Self-Deception and Belief Attribution."

44. Fingarette, *Self-Deception,* 66–67.

45. Ibid., 71.

46. Ibid., 38–39.

47. Ibid., 87, emphasis in original.

48. Kent Bach makes this criticism, observing that Fingarette's model is persuasive so far as it goes, but it gives "no explicit indication of what sort of proposition . . . self-deception is supposed to be about" ("An Analysis of Self-Deception," *Philosophy and Phenomenological Research* 41 [1981]: 352).

49. Robert Audi, "Self-Deception and Practical Reasoning," *Canadian Journal of Philosophy* 19, no. 2 (June 1989): 249. See also "Epistemic Disavowals and Self-Deception," *The Personalist* 57 (1976): 378–85; "Self-Deception, Action, and Will," *Erkenntnis* 18 (1982): 133–58; and "Self-Deception and Rationality," in *Self-Deception and Self-Understanding,* ed. Martin, 169–94.

50. Audi, "Self-Deception and Practical Reasoning," 248.

CHAPTER 4: THE SPIRIT IS WILLING

1. The term *akrasia* is difficult to translate into English. While it has been typically translated as "moral weakness" or "weakness of will," it has also been rendered "incontinence," "lack of self-restraint," and "weakness of character."

2. This formulation is adapted from Donald Davidson's rendering in "How Is Weakness of the Will Possible?" in *Moral Concepts,* ed. Joel Feinberg (Oxford: Oxford University Press, 1970), 95.

3. Socrates' argument here, specifically as regards his use of hedonism, is controversial and has been the subject of much scholarly dispute. For further discussion see J. P. Sullivan, "The Hedonism in Plato's *Protagoras,*" *Phronesis* 6, no. 1 (1961): 10–28; Gerasimos Santas, "Plato's *Protagoras* and Explanations of Weakness," *Philosophical Review* 75 (1966): 3–33; and David Gallop, "The Socratic Parodox in the *Protagoras,*" *Phronesis* 9 (1964): 117–29.

4. Plato, *Protagoras,* trans. W. K. Guthrie, in *The Collected Dialogues of Plato,* eds. Edith Hamilton and Huntington Cairns (Princeton: Princeton University Press, 1961), 349.

5. I shall refer to this thesis as the Socratic view, though this is potentially misleading. Determining just what views are to be attributed to Socrates rather than Plato (and vice versa) is a tricky matter, about which scholars disagree. The principal reason for my labeling the skeptical thesis "Socratic" is that the later Plato seems to allow for the possibility of weakness of will.

6. Aristotle, *Nicomachean Ethics,* trans. W. D. Ross, in *The Basic Works of Aristotle,* ed. Richard McKeon (New York: Random House, 1941), 1038.

7. For helpful treatments of Aristotle's doctrine (which is as controversial as Plato's) see James Walsh, *Aristotle's Conception of Moral Weakness* (New York: Columbia University Press, 1963); W. F. Hardie, "Aristotle on Moral Weakness," in *Weakness of Will,* ed. Geoffrey Mortimore (London: Macmillan and Company, 1971); and David L. Schaefer, "Wisdom and Morality: Aristotle's Account of *Akrasia,*" *Polity* 21, no. 2 (winter, 1988).

8. Aristotle, *Nicomachean Ethics,* 1049.

9. Ibid., 1050.

10. Ibid., 1052.

11. Ibid., 1037.

12. Gilbert Ryle, *The Concept of Mind* (London: Hutchinson and Co., 1949), chaps. 2 and 5.

13. Ibid., 118.

14. See R. M. Hare, *The Language of Morals* (Oxford: Oxford University Press, 1952) and *Freedom and Reason* (Oxford: Oxford University Press, 1963).

15. *Freedom and Reason,* 81.

16. Ibid., 83, emphasis in original.

17. I borrow this criticism of Hare from Robert Dunn, *The Possibility of Weakness of the Will* (Indianapolis: Hackett Publishing Company, 1987), 10.

18. Steven Lukes, "Moral Weakness," *The Philosophical Quarterly* 15 (1965): 112.

19. See Davidson's "How Is Weakness of the Will Possible?" in *Moral Concepts,* ed. Joel Feinberg (Oxford: Oxford University Press, 1970) and "Intending" in *Essays on Actions and Events,* ed. Donald Davidson (Oxford: Oxford University Press, 1980).

20. Davidson, *Essays on Actions and Events,* 96–99.

21. Davidson, *Moral Concepts,* 112.

22. Ibid.

23. Ibid., 112–13.

24. I borrow this criticism from Gary Watson. See his "Skepticism About Weakness of Will," *Philosophical Review* 86 (1977): 319.

25. Ibid., 330.

26. Ibid., 332, emphasis in original.

27. John King-Farlow, "*Akrasia,* Self-Mastery and the Master Self," *Pacific Philosophical Quarterly* 62 (1981): 52.

28. Ibid., 51, emphasis in original.

29. Michael Stocker, "Desiring the Bad: An Essay in Moral Psychology," *Journal of Philosophy* 76, no. 12 (1979): 745.

30. Ibid.

31. David Pears, "How Easy Is *Akrasia?*" *Philosophia* 11 (1982): 48.

32. Ibid., 47.

33. Ibid., 48.

34. As we saw in the previous chapter, Pears's account of self-deception *is* compartmentalist in nature. But his account of *akrasia* is not necessarily committed to such a model.

35. Matt. 26:41.

36. Douglas Moo, *The Epistle to the Romans* (Grand Rapids: Eerdmans, 1996), 448. For further criticisms of the "postconversion" view, see: F. Godet, *Commentary on the Epistle to the Romans,* trans. A. Cusin (Grand Rapids: Zondervan, 1969), 280–94, and F. Leroy Forlines, *The Randall House Bible Commentary: Romans* (Nashville: Randall House, 1987), 178–97.

37. Martin Luther, *Lectures on Romans,* trans. Wilhelm Pauck (Philadelphia: The Westminster Press, 1961), 208.

38. Martin Lloyd-Jones, *Romans: Chapters 7:1–8:4* (Grand Rapids: Zondervan, 1973), 198. For further criticisms of the "preconversion" interpretation of this passage, see: F. F. Bruce, *The Letter of Paul to the Romans* (Grand Rapids: Eerdmans, 1985), 143–45; Matthew Henry, *Commentary on the Whole Bible,* vol. 6 (McLean, Va.: MacDonald Publishing Company, n.d.), 411–12; Charles Hodge, *Commentary on the Epistle to the Romans* (Grand Rapids: Eerdmans, 1950); and John Murray, *The Epistle to the Romans,* vol. 1 (Grand Rapids: Eerdmans, 1959), 256–73.

39. See Charles Hodge's discussion of this point in his *Commentary on the Epistle to the Romans,* 239–40.

40. Naturally, defenders of the preconversion interpretation insist that against all appearances, Paul speaks not for himself (in his current regenerate state) here. Hodge insightfully replies that this is "to suppose him to do what he does nowhere else in any of his writings, and what is entirely foreign to his whole spirit and manner" (*Commentary on the Epistle to the Romans,* 241).

41. Some might find this line of argument objectionable because of the deference it pays to personal experience. But since Paul's discussion in this passage constitutes a sort of moral phenomenology, which is an empirical

matter, it is appropriate that one's interpretation of it be tested against common experience. And I think that the struggle and inner conflict described by Paul in this passage is something with which many mature Christians can readily identify.

42. Heb. 12:4.

43. 1 Peter 2:11.

CHAPTER 5: THE NOW AND THE NOT YET

1. Rom. 3:23.

2. Isa. 53:6.

3. Ps. 14:3.

4. Ps. 51:5.

5. Augustine, *Enchiridion,* trans. Henry Paolucci (Chicago: Henry Regnery Company, 1961), 58.

6. Thomas Aquinas, *Summa Theologica,* trans. English Dominican Fathers (New York: Benziger Brothers, Inc., 1947), vol. 1 (1.2.82.2), 956.

7. Martin Luther, *The Bondage of the Will,* in *Erasmus-Luther: Discourse on Free Will,* trans. and ed. Ernst F. Winter (New York: Frederick Ungar Publishing Co., Inc., 1961), 129.

8. John Calvin, *Institutes of the Christian Religion* (Philadelphia: Westminster Press, 1960), vol. 2 (2.1.8), 251.

9. Ibid.

10. Ibid., (2.1.9), 253.

11. Jonathan Edwards, *The Works of Jonathan Edwards,* vol. 1 (Edinburgh: Banner of Truth Trust, 1974), 149.

12. Ibid., 150.

13. John Wesley, *Original Sin,* in *The Works of John Wesley,* vol. 9 (Grand Rapids: Zondervan, 1872), 367.

14. Rom. 5:18.

15. Amelie Rorty, *Mind in Action* (Boston: Beacon Press, 1988), chap. 13.

16. Ibid., 259.

17. Aristotle, *Nicomachean Ethics,* trans. W. D. Ross, in *The Basic Works of Aristotle,* ed., Richard McKeon (New York: Random House, 1941), book 3.

18. Rorty, *Mind in Action,* 260.

19. Aristotle, *Nicomachean Ethics,* 955.

20. I know of a person, for example, who seemed doomed to failure in resisting the temptation of pornography. He finally overcame it when he took steps to avoid the temptation itself by taking a different route to work, as his usual route led him by a pornographic magazine stand. While this did not solve his problem altogether, it immensely improved his progress.

21. I would like to think that reading this book might prove helpful to some in this regard, though it was not my primary aim for this volume to be a self-help manual.

22. Rorty, *Mind in Action,* 245.

23. Roberto Assagioli elaborates at length on this technique, as in the following excerpt: "Picture to yourself as vividly as possible the loss of opportunity, the damage, the pain to yourself and others which has actu-

ally occurred, and which might again occur, as a result of the present lack of strength of your will. . . . Allow the feelings which these recollections and forecasts arouse to affect you intensely. Then let them evoke in you a strong urge to change your condition.

"Picture to yourself as vividly as possible all the *advantages* that an effective will can bring to you; all the benefits, opportunities, and satisfactions which will come from it to yourself and others. . . . Allow the feelings aroused by these anticipations to have full sway. . . ." (*The Act of Will* [New York: The Viking Press, 1973] 36).

24. Phil. 4:8.

25. Aristotle writes that "some men become temperate and good-tempered, others self-indulgent and irascible, by behaving in one way or the other in the appropriate circumstances. Thus, in one word, states of character arise out of like activities" (*Nicomachean Ethics,* 953). And William James soberly warns, "Could the young but realize how soon they will become mere walking bundles of habits, they would give more heed to their conduct while in the plastic state. We are spinning our own fates, good or evil, and never to be undone. Every smallest stroke of virtue or of vice leaves its never so little scar" (William James, *The Principles of Psychology,* vol. 1 [New York: Dover Publications, Inc., 1950], 127).

26. William James, *The Principles of Psychology,* 126.

27. For a powerful argument for the importance of practicing the spiritual disciplines (i.e., prayer, meditation, fasting, silence, frugality, study, etc.) and for their value in developing self-control, see Dallas Willard's *The Spirit of the Disciplines* (San Francisco: HarperCollins, 1988). Willard assumes, in agreement with my account, that the virtue of self-control is an acquired skill.

28. Robert Roberts, "Will Power and the Virtues," *The Virtues: Contemporary Essays on Moral Character,* eds. Robert Kruschwitz and Robert Roberts (Belmont, Calif.: Wadsworth Publishing Co., 1987), 13.

29. Ibid., 12.

30. E. Boyd Barrett, *Strength of the Will and How to Develop It* (New York: Richard R. Smith, 1931), as quoted in Assagioli, *The Act of Will,* 40–41.

31. 2 Tim. 1:7.

32. 1 Peter 5:8–9.

33. Rorty, *Mind in Action,* 258.

34. Matt. 5:48.

35. Roman Catechism, 2.2.50.

36. For a helpful summary of the Roman Catholic doctrine of justification and sanctifying grace, see Ludwig Ott's *Fundamentals of Catholic Dogma,* trans. Patrick Lynch (Rockford, Ill.: Tan Books and Publishers, Inc., 1974), 250–59.

37. John Calvin speaks for most Protestant theologians when he says that sanctification "does not take place in one moment or one day or one year; but through continual and sometimes even slow advances God wipes out in his elect the corruptions of the flesh, cleanses them of guilt, consecrates them to himself as temples renewing all their minds to true purity that they

may practice repentance throughout their lives and know that this warfare will end only at death" (*Institutes of the Christian Religion*, vol. 1, 601).

38. For example, see L. Berkhof, *Systematic Theology* (Grand Rapids: Eerdmans, 1941), 527–44, and John Murray, *The Collected Writings of John Murray*, vol. 2 (Edinburgh: The Banner of Truth Trust, 1977), chaps. 21–23.

39. For dispensationalist discussions of sanctification, see Lewis Chafer, *Systematic Theology*, vol. 2 (Dallas: Dallas Theological Seminary, 1947–48), and Charles Ryrie, *Balancing the Christian Life* (Chicago: Moody Press, 1969), chaps. 6–7.

40. John Walvoord, "The Augustinian-Dispensational Perspective," in *Five Views on Sanctification*, ed. M. E. Dieter et al. (Grand Rapids: Zondervan, 1987), 225.

41. Charles Ryrie typifies the dispensational approach in maintaining that the believer's responsibility in sanctification is dedication or yielding oneself to God. However, the yielding process is piecemeal. As Ryrie explains, "to dedicate in some area or in relation to some thing will . . . mean that only that area or thing in life has been yielded to the Lord's control. Then in the course of time another problem or decision will face the person, and he will have to decide whether or not to yield to the Lord's will in that respect. Then another choice will arise . . . and so on and on through life," *Balancing the Christian Life*, 78–79.

42. Wesley, *The Works of John Wesley*, vol. 6, 412.

43. Ibid., 417. Wesley was convinced that he personally knew many persons who had attained entire sanctification. See *Christian Perfection as Taught by John Wesley*, ed. J. A. Wood (Chicago: The Christian Witness Co., 1885), sec. 12.

44. For Assemblies of God writers of this persuasion, see Myer Pearlman, *Knowing the Doctrines of the Bible* (Springfield, Mo.: The Gospel Publishing House, 1937), chap. 8, and P. C. Nelson, *Bible Doctrines* (Springfield, Mo.: Gospel Publishing House, 1948), chap. 9. For examples of the Keswickian approach, see Steven Barabas, *So Great a Salvation* (London: Marshall, Morgan and Scott, 1952), and J. Robertson McQuilkin's essay "The Keswick Perspective," in *Five Views on Sanctification*, 151–83.

CHAPTER 6: CHEATING AT THE GOODNESS STAKES

1. The term "teleological" is derived from the Greek word *telos*, which means "end, purpose, goal or function."

2. John Stuart Mill, *Utilitarianism*, in *Mill's Ethical Writings*, ed. J. B. Schneewind (New York: The MacMillan Company, 1965), 281.

3. See Epicurus' *Letters, Principal Doctrines, and Vatican Sayings*, trans. Russel M. Geer (New York: Macmillan/Library of the Liberal Arts, 1964).

4. The principal work of Bentham's in which his utilitarian moral theory is articulated is his *The Principles of Morals and Legislation* (1789).

5. *Mill's Ethical Writings*, 284.

6. Ibid., 298.

7. Ibid., 291.

8. Immanuel Kant, "What is Enlightenment?" in *Foundations of the Metaphysics of Morals*, trans. Lewis White Beck (Indianapolis: The Bobbs-Mer-

rill Company, Inc., 1959), 91. Kant understands self-incurred tutelage as "man's inability to make use of his understanding without direction from another." The escape from this, Kant maintained, was essential "chiefly in matters of religion because our rulers have no interest in playing the guardian with respect to the arts and sciences and also because religious incompetence is not only the most harmful but also the most degrading of all" (ibid).

9. Kant, *Foundations of the Metaphysics of Morals,* 9.

10. Ibid., 39.

11. Ibid., 47.

12. Kantian moral theory enjoys many strengths. First, it takes notions of moral duty and obligation seriously. Second, it sees morality as essentially rational. Third, it avoids some of the pitfalls of consequentialist theories such as utilitarianism, particularly as regards matters of justice. And from a Christian perspective the theory has an additional virtue. As Kant himself notes, the categorical imperative captures much of the spirit of the Golden Rule.

However, there are also problems with the Kantian approach. Not the least of these is its unyielding rigor. For instance, since we cannot universalize lying, does this mean during World War II, those harboring Jews had a duty to tell the Nazis the truth if they were asked whether they were doing so? This seems unreasonable. And if a Kantian allows for exceptions by making the maxim in question more specific (e.g., "one may lie just in those cases where doing so will save an innocent human life"), then the question arises, How specific are we to make the imperative that will be tested? Couldn't such qualifiers be used to justify lying to just this person or cheating on just this particular test?

13. Aristotle, *Nicomachean Ethics,* trans. W. D. Ross, in *The Basic Works of Aristotle,* ed. Richard McKeon (New York: Random House, 1941), 957.

14. The person-orientedness of Aristotle's ethics is certainly one of the strengths of the theory, as is its emphasis on social context in defining virtue. Here Aristotle's approach avoids some of the pitfalls of utilitarian and Kantian approaches, which emphasize moral evaluation of acts rather than persons. However, a virtue-based approach also has unique shortcomings. First, it may show us what sorts of persons we should be and the sorts of character traits we should strive to develop, but it fails to give guidance on particular issues in ethics, such as regards the morality of abortion, war, capital punishment, affirmative action, and so forth. In this sense, the theory is incomplete as a moral philosophy. Furthermore, it is not always easy to tell just what the mean is between two vices. What seems moderate to one person might seem extreme to another.

15. I am indebted to Henry Krabbendam at Covenant College for this idea.

16. Kantian ethics accords well with some basic biblical injunctions relating to the importance of universalizability, respect for others, and a good will. As Kant himself notes, the categorical imperative captures the spirit of the Golden Rule, which Jesus offered as a basic moral principle. To behave

toward others as you would have them behave toward you is in a sense to apply the first version of the categorical imperative. Similarly, biblical exhortations that Christians be loving, kind, patient, and gentle toward one another are consonant with the imperative to treat others as ends. Finally, the importance of pure motives or a good will is emphasized throughout the Scriptures (i.e., Ps. 51:10; Ps. 139:23–24; James 2:4; 1 John 2:9–10). In these respects, a Kantian approach seems to highlight significant elements of biblical morality.

17. Fyodor Dostoevski, *The Brothers Karamazov,* trans. Constance Garnett (New York: William Heinemann, Ltd., 1945), 37–38.

18. Plato, *The Republic,* trans. Paul Shorey, in *The Collected Dialogues of Plato,* eds. Edith Hamilton and Huntington Cairns (Princeton: Princeton University Press, 1961), 607–8.

19. Ibid., 608.

20. Note that of the three species of hypocrisy distinguished in chapter 2, one of these—that consisting in a cognitive-behavioral conflict—is not subject to the latter sorts of utilitarian criticisms just discussed; that is, those based on the effects that hypocrisy has on others.

21. Christine McKinnon, "Hypocrisy, with a Note on Integrity," *American Philosophical Quarterly* 28, no. 4 (October 1991): 326.

22. Eva F. Kittay, "Hypocrisy," *Encyclopedia of Ethics,* eds. Lawrence C. Becker and Charlotte Becker, vol. 1 (New York: Garland Publishing, Inc., 1992), 285.

23. Roger Crisp and Christopher Cowton, "Hypocrisy and Moral Seriousness," *American Philosophical Quarterly* 31, no. 4 (October 1994): 347.

24. This is one of the important insights made by Christine McKinnon in her "Hypocrisy, with a Note on Integrity," 329.

25. I borrow this definition from Robert Roberts. See his "Sense of Humor as a Christian Virtue," *Faith and Philosophy* 7, no. 2 (April 1990): 190.

26. Thomas Aquinas, *Summa Theologica,* trans. English Dominican Fathers (New York: Benziger Brothers, Inc., 1947), vol. 2 (2.2.111.1), 1669.

27. On the whole matter of common courtesy and routine politeness, see Piers Benn, "What Is Wrong with Hypocrisy?" 230–32.

28. Ibid., 232.

29. McKinnon, "Hypocrisy, with a Note on Integrity," 326.

30. See Ronald Dworkin, *Law's Empire* (Cambridge, Mass: Harvard University Press, 1986), chaps. 6–7.

31. My definition of integrity here is at variance with that of Christine McKinnon, who doubts whether it is even a first-order virtue. She maintains that "integrity is rather like a second-order desire that all one's first order desires be consistent with one's considered evaluations of what is worthy." The reason for her skepticism about whether integrity is a virtue is that "it is not the kind of thing that gives rise to specific first-order desires or motivations" ("Hypocrisy, with a Note on Integrity," 328).

32. This also helps to explain why Jesus' rebukes of the Pharisees were so severe.

33. Hannah Arendt, *On Revolution* (New York: The Viking Press, Inc., 1963), 99.

34. Francois de La Rochefoucauld in *Reflections, or Sentences and Moral Maxims* (New York: H. M. Caldwell Co., 1900), maxim 218, 64.

35. See C. S. Lewis, *Mere Christianity* (New York: Macmillan, 1952), chap. 1.

36. John Calvin, *Institutes of the Christian Religion*, vol. 1 (1.4.4), trans. F. L. Battles (Philadelphia: The Westminster Press, 1960), 50–51.

Chapter 7: At Least I'm Not a Hypocrite

1. Keith Lehrer is a notable contemporary example. See his "Why Not Skepticism?" *Philosophical Forum* 2, no. 3 (1971): 283–98. This is the best defense of global skepticism that I have seen to date.

2. Because the term "exclusive" may misleadingly suggest elitism or a certain narrowness of perspective, some contemporary exclusivists prefer the term "particularist" to describe themselves. Examples include Alister McGrath, R. Douglas Geivett, and W. Gary Phillips, whose particularist perspectives are articulated in essays collected in *More Than One Way?* eds. Dennis L. Okholm and Timothy R. Phillips (Grand Rapids: Zondervan, 1995).

3. In addition to *More Than One Way?* see Clark Pinnock's *A Wideness in God's Mercy* (Grand Rapids: Zondervan, 1992), and Ronald Nash's *Is Jesus the Only Savior?* (Grand Rapids: Zondervan, 1994).

4. The oldest formal school of skeptical thought is Pyrrhonism, associated with the teachings of Pyrrho of Elis (360–270 B.C.). The most famous of ancient skeptics, Sextus Empiricus, championed this brand of skepticism, which was revived in the modern period by such thinkers as Michel de Montaigne and David Hume.

5. I am using the term "exclusivism" to denote the view that Christianity is the one true religion, in contrast to religious pluralism which denies this. There is actually a third view known as "inclusivism" (defended by Clark Pinnock, among others) which claims a middle ground between these two perspectives. The Christian inclusivist maintains that Christianity is the one true religion but that some other religions are imperfect approximations of this one truth, that salvation is found in Christ alone, and that persons of other faiths may unwittingly come to God through him, though they do not explicitly believe in him. I neglect dwelling on this important third view only to avoid complicating the present discussion, not because I do not think that there is much to recommend this subtle position. For the sake of treating skeptical objections from hypocrisy, we may properly group inclusivists with exclusivists, for both maintain—and this is the crucial point in the present context—that Christianity is the one true (or truest) religion. For expositions of religious inclusivism, see Pinnock's *A Wideness in God's Mercy* and John Sanders' *No Other Name* (Grand Rapids: Zondervan, 1992).

6. Hick's position is similar to that of Paul Tillich, who conceives faith as ultimate concern and God as the mysterious ground of all being. See Tillich's *Dynamics of Faith* (New York: HarperCollins Publishers, 1957).

7. John Hick, "The Non-Absoluteness of Christianity," in *The Myth of Christian Uniqueness,* eds. John Hick and Paul F. Knitter (Maryknoll, N. Y.: Orbis Books, 1989), 23.

8. Ibid., 24.

9. Ibid., 30.

10. Ibid.

11. In a later article titled "A Pluralist View" (in *More Than One Way?*), Hick softens his claim somewhat, saying "[r]ather than suggest a comparative quantification of a kind that is not in fact possible, I propose the more modest and negative conclusion, that it is not possible to establish the moral superiority of the adherents of any one of the great traditions over the rest" (p. 41). But in spite of this admission, Hick insinuates that Christianity is on a moral par with other religions, a claim which he cannot justifiably make if he is to be consistent with his stated skepticism about making such comparisons.

12. There is some dispute among Hume scholars as to whether in fact Philo speaks for Hume in the *Dialogues,* as opposed to one of the other characters (Cleanthes, Demea, and Pamphilus) or some combination thereof. However, I am in agreement with Norman Kemp Smith when he remarks that "Philo, from start to finish, represents Hume." For his defense of this interpretation, see his introduction to Hume's *Dialogues Concerning Natural Religion* (Indianapolis: Bobbs-Merrill Publishing Co., 1947), 57–75.

13. Ibid., 220.

14. Ibid., 221.

15. Ibid., 222.

16. Ibid.

17. Ibid., 223.

18. Ibid.

19. Ibid., 224.

20. Bertrand Russell, *Why I Am Not a Christian* (New York: Simon and Schuster, 1957), 15.

21. For an excellent recent defense of religious exclusivism, see Alvin Plantinga's "A Defense of Religious Exclusivism," in *Philosophy of Religion,* ed. Louis P. Pojman (Belmont, Calif.: Wadsworth Publishing Co., 1994), 529–44.

22. C. S. Lewis, *Mere Christianity* (New York: Macmillan, 1952), 85–86.

23. Luke 6:43.

24. 1 John 3:9.

25. James 2:14–24.

26. It is a paradoxical yet, I believe, irresistible conclusion that given these aspects of Christian doctrine, the problem of hypocrisy actually confirms the truth of Christian theism.

Bibliography

Aquinas, Thomas. *Summa Theologica*. Vols. 1 and 2. Translated by the English Dominican Fathers. New York: Benziger Brothers, 1947.

Arendt, Hannah. *On Revolution*. New York: Viking Press, 1963.

Aristotle. *The Basic Works of Aristotle*. Edited by Richard McKeon. New York: Random House, 1941.

Assagioli, Roberto. *The Act of Will*. New York: Viking Press, 1973.

Audi, Robert. "Epistemic Disavowals and Self-Deception." *The Personalist* 57 (1976): 378–85.

————. "Self-Deception, Action, and Will." *Erkenntnis* 18 (1982): 133–58.

————. "Self-Deception and Practical Reasoning." *Canadian Journal of Philosophy* 19 (1989): 247–66.

————. "Self-Deception and Rationality." In *Self-Deception and Self-Understanding*, edited by Mike W. Martin, 169–94. Lawrence, Kans.: University Press of Kansas, 1985.

Augustine, Saint. *Enchiridion*. Translated by Henry Paolucci. Chicago: Henry Regnery, 1961.

Bach, Kent. "An Analysis of Self-Deception." *Philosophy and Phenomenological Research* 41 (1981): 351–70.

Barabas, Steven. *So Great a Salvation*. London: Marshall, Morgan and Scott, 1952.

Barrett, E. Boyd. *Strength of the Will and How to Develop It*. New York: Richard R. Smith, 1931.

Benn, Piers. "What Is Wrong with Hypocrisy?" *International Journal of Moral and Social Studies* 8 (1993): 223–35.

Bentham, Jeremy. *The Principles of Morals and Legislation*. New York: Hafner, 1948.

Berkhof, Louis. *Systematic Theology*. Grand Rapids: Eerdmans, 1941.

Bruce, F. F. *The Letter of Paul to the Romans*. Grand Rapids: Eerdmans, 1985.

Butler, Joseph. *Fifteen Sermons*. London: G. Bell and Sons, 1964.

Calvin, John. *Institutes of the Christian Religion*. Vols. 1 and 2. Translated by F. L. Battles. Philadelphia: Westminster Press, 1960.

Canfield, John V., and Don F. Gustavson. "Self-Deception." *Analysis* 23 (1962): 32–36.

Chafer, Lewis. *Systematic Theology.* Vol. 2. Dallas: Dallas Theological Seminary, 1947–48.

Champlin, T. S. "Deceit, Deception, and the Self-Deceiver." *Philosophical Investigations* 17 (1994): 53–58.

Crisp, Roger, and Christopher Cowton. "Hypocrisy and Moral Seriousness." *American Philosophical Quarterly* 31 (1994): 343–49.

da Costa, Newton, and Steven French. "Belief, Contradiction and the Logic of Self-Deception." *American Philosophical Quarterly* 27 (1990): 179–97.

Davidson, Donald. "How Is Weakness of the Will Possible?" In *Moral Concepts,* edited by Joel Feinberg, 93–113. Oxford: Oxford University Press, 1970.

———, ed. *Essays on Actions and Events.* Oxford: Oxford University Press, 1980.

Demos, Raphael. "Lying to Oneself." *The Journal of Philosophy* 57 (1960): 588–95.

Descartes, Rene. *The Philosophical Works of Descartes.* Vol. 1. Edited by E. S. Haldane and G. R. Ross. Cambridge: University Press, 1968.

Dostoevski, Fyodor. *The Brothers Karamazov.* Translated by Constance Garnett. New York: William Heinemann, 1945.

———. *Crime and Punishment.* New York: Dell, 1959.

Dunn, Robert. *The Possibility of Weakness of the Will.* Indianapolis: Hackett, 1987.

Dworkin, R. M. *Law's Empire.* Cambridge, Mass.: Harvard University Press, 1986.

Edwards, Jonathan. *The Works of Jonathan Edwards.* Vol. 1. Edinburgh: Banner of Truth Trust, 1974.

Epicurus. *Letters, Principal Doctrines, and Vatican Sayings.* Translated by Russel M. Geer. New York: Macmillan, 1964.

Fingarette, Herbert. *Self-Deception.* London: Routledge and Kegan Paul, 1969.

Forlines, F. Leroy. *The Randall House Bible Commentary: Romans.* Nashville: Randall House, 1987.

Gallop, David. "The Socratic Paradox in the Protagoras." *Phronesis* 9 (1964): 117–29.

Godet, F. *Commentary on the Epistle to the Romans.* Translated by A. Cusin. Grand Rapids: Zondervan, 1969.

Haight, M. R. *A Study of Self-Deception.* Sussex: Harvester Press, 1980.

Hales, Steven. "Self-Deception and Belief Attribution." *Synthese* 101 (1994): 273–89.

Hamlyn, D. W. "Self-Deception." *Proceedings of the Aristotelian Society* 45 (1971): 45–60.

Hardie, W. F. "Aristotle on Moral Weakness." In *Weakness of Will,* edited by Geoffrey Mortimore, 69–94. London: Macmillan, 1971.

Hare, R. M. *Freedom and Reason.* Oxford: Oxford University Press, 1963.

———. *The Language of Morals.* Oxford: Oxford University Press, 1952.

Hegel, Georg Wilhelm Friedrich. *Phenomenology of Spirit.* Translated by A. V. Miller. Oxford: Oxford University Press, 1977.

————. *Philosophy of Right.* Translated by T. M. Knox. Oxford: Oxford University Press, 1952.

Henry, Matthew. *Commentary on the Whole Bible.* Vol. 6. McLean, Va.: MacDonald, n.d.

Hick, John, and Paul F. Knitter, eds. *The Myth of Christian Uniqueness.* Maryknoll, New York: Orbis Books, 1989.

Hodge, Charles. *Commentary on the Epistle to the Romans.* Grand Rapids: Eerdmans, 1950.

Hume, David. *Dialogues Concerning Natural Religion.* Indianapolis: Bobbs-Merrill, 1947.

James, William. *The Principles of Psychology.* Vol. 1. New York: Dover Publications, 1950.

Johnston, Mark. "Self-Deception and the Nature of Mind." In *Perspectives on Self-Deception,* edited by B. P. McLaughlin and A. O. Rorty, 63–91. Berkeley: University of California Press, 1988.

Jones, David. "Pervasive Self-Deception." *The Southern Journal of Philosophy* 27 (1989): 217–37.

Kant, Immanuel. *Foundations of the Metaphysics of Morals.* Translated by Lewis White Beck. Indianapolis: The Bobbs-Merrill Company, Inc., 1959.

King-Farlow, John. "*Akrasia,* Self-Mastery and the Master Self." *Pacific Philosophical Quarterly* 62 (1981): 47–60.

————. "Self-Deceivers and Sartrian Seducers." *Analysis* 23 (1963): 131–36.

Kipp, David. "On Self-Deception." *Philosophical Quarterly* 30 (1980): 305–17.

Kittay, Eva F. "Hypocrisy." In *Encyclopedia of Ethics.* Vol. 1. Edited by Lawrence C. Becker and Charlotte Becker, 582–87. New York: Garland Publishing, 1992.

————. "On Hypocrisy." *Metaphilosophy* 13 (1982): 277–89.

La Rochefoucauld, Francois. *Reflections, or Sentences and Moral Maxims.* New York: H. M. Caldwell Co., 1900.

Lehrer, Keith. "Why Not Skepticism?" *The Philosophical Forum* 2 (1971): 283–98.

Lewis, C. S. *Mere Christianity.* New York: Macmillan, 1952.

Lloyd-Jones, Martin. *Romans: Chapters 7:1–8:4.* Grand Rapids: Zondervan, 1973.

Locke, John. *Essay Concerning Human Understanding.* Oxford: Oxford University Press, 1975.

Lukes, Steven. "Moral Weakness." *The Philosophical Quarterly* 15 (1965): 104–14.

Luther, Martin. *The Bondage of the Will.* In *Erasmus-Luther: Discourse on Free Will.* Translated and edited by Ernst F. Winter. New York: Frederick Ungar Publishing, Inc., 1961.

————. *Lectures on Romans.* Translated by Wilhelm Pauck. Philadelphia: Westminster Press, 1961.

Mandeville, Bernard. *The Fable of the Bees.* Oxford: Clarendon Press, 1957.

McKinnon, Christine. "Hypocrisy, with a Note on Integrity." *American Philosophical Quarterly* 28 (1991): 321–30.

McQuilkin, J. Robertson. "The Keswick Perspective." In *Five Views on Sanctification,* edited by M. E. Dieter et al. Grand Rapids: Zondervan, 1987.

Mele, Alfred. "Real Self-Deception." *Behavioral and Brain Sciences* 20 (1997): 91–102.

———. "Recent Work on Self-Deception." *American Philosophical Quarterly* 24 (1987): 1–17.

———. "Self-Deception." *Philosophical Quarterly* 33 (1983): 165–77.

Mill, John Stuart. *Utilitarianism.* In *Mill's Ethical Writings,* edited by J. B. Schneewind. New York: Macmillan, 1965.

Moliere, Jean Baptist Poquelin. *The Misanthrope and Tartuffe.* Translated by Richard Wilbur. New York: Harcourt, Brace, and World, 1954.

Moo, Douglas J. *The Epistle to the Romans.* Grand Rapids: Eerdmans, 1996.

Murray, John. *The Collected Writings of John Murray.* Vol. 2. Edinburgh: Banner of Truth Trust, 1977.

———. *The Epistle to the Romans.* Vol. 1. Grand Rapids: Eerdmans, 1959.

Nash, Ronald. *Is Jesus the Only Savior?* Grand Rapids: Zondervan, 1994.

Nelson, P. C. *Bible Doctrines.* Springfield, Mo.: Gospel Publishing, 1948.

Nietzsche, Friedrich. *The Genealogy of Morals and Beyond Good and Evil.* In *Basic Writings of Nietzsche,* translated and edited by Walter Kaufmann. New York: Modern Library, 1968.

Okholm, Dennis L., and Timothy R. Phillips, eds. *More Than One Way?* Grand Rapids: Zondervan, 1995.

Ott, Ludwig. *Fundamentals of Catholic Dogma.* Translated by Patrick Lynch. Rockford, Ill.: Tan Books and Publishers, 1974.

Paluch, Stanley. "Self-Deception." *Inquiry* 10 (1967): 268–78.

Pearlman, Myer. *Knowing the Doctrines of the Bible.* Springfield, Mo.: Gospel Publishing, 1937.

Pears, David. "How Easy Is *Akrasia?*" *Philosophia* 11 (1982): 33–50.

———. *Motivated Irrationality.* Oxford: Oxford University Press, 1984.

Penelhum, Terence. "Pleasure and Falsity." In *Philosophy of Mind,* edited by Stuart Hampshire, 242–66. New York: Harper and Row, 1966.

Peterman, James. "Self-Deception and the Problem of Avoidance." *Southern Journal of Philosophy* 21 (1983): 565–73.

Pinnock, Clark. *A Wideness in God's Mercy.* Grand Rapids: Zondervan, 1992.

Plantinga, Alvin. "A Defense of Religious Exclusivism." In *Philosophy of Religion,* edited by Louis P. Pojman, 529–44. Belmont, Calif.: Wadsworth, 1994.

Plato. *The Collected Dialogues of Plato.* Edited by Edith Hamilton and Huntington Cairns. Princeton: Princeton University Press, 1961.

Pugmire, David. "'Strong' Self-Deception." *Inquiry* 12 (1969): 339–61.

Roberts, Robert. "Sense of Humor as a Christian Virtue." *Faith and Philosophy* 7 (1990): 177–92.

———. "Will Power and the Virtues." In *The Virtues: Contemporary Essays on Moral Character,* edited by Robert Kruschwitz and Robert Roberts. Belmont, Calif.: Wadsworth Publishing, 1987.

Rorty, Amelie O. "Belief and Self-Deception." *Inquiry* 15 (1972): 387–410.

————. "The Deceptive Self: Liars, Layers, and Lairs." In *Perspectives on Self-Deception,* edited by Brian P. McLaughlin and Amelie O. Rorty, 11–28. Berkeley: University of California Press, 1988.

————. *Mind in Action.* Boston: Beacon Press, 1988.

————. "Self-Deception, *Akrasia,* and Irrationality." *Social Science Information* 19 (1980): 905–22.

————. "User-Friendly Self-Deception." *Philosophy* 69 (1994): 211–28.

Russell, Bertrand. *Why I Am Not a Christian.* New York: Simon and Schuster, 1957.

Ryle, Gilbert. *The Concept of Mind.* London: Hutchinson and Co., 1949.

Ryrie, Charles. *Balancing the Christian Life.* Chicago: Moody Press, 1969.

Sanders, John. *No Other Name.* Grand Rapids: Zondervan, 1992.

Santas, Gerasimos. "Plato's Protagoras and Explanations of Weakness." *The Philosophical Review* 75 (1966): 3–33.

Sartre, Jean Paul. *Being and Nothingness.* Translated by Hazel E. Barnes. New York: Washington Square Press, 1956.

Schaefer, David L. "Wisdom and Morality: Aristotle's Account of *Akrasia.*" *Polity* 21 (1988): 221–51

Sklar, Judith N. *Ordinary Vices.* Cambridge: Belknap Press, 1984.

Siegler, F. A. "Demos on Lying to Oneself." *Journal of Philosophy* 59 (1962): 469–75.

Spiegel, James. "Socrates: A Messianic Type for the Gentiles." *Philosophia Christi* 18 (1995): 43–64.

Stocker, Michael. "Desiring the Bad: An Essay in Moral Psychology." *The Journal of Philosophy* 76 (1979): 738–53.

Sullivan, J. P. "The Hedonism in Plato's Protagoras." *Phronesis* 6 (1961): 10–28.

Szabados, Bela. "Hypocrisy." *Canadian Journal of Philosophy* 9 (1979): 195–210.

Tillich, Paul. *Dynamics of Faith.* New York: HarperCollins, 1957.

Walsh, James. *Aristotle's Conception of Moral Weakness.* New York: Columbia University Press, 1963.

Walvoord, John. "The Augustinian-Dispensational Perspective." In *Five Views on Sanctification,* edited by M. E. Dieter et al. Grand Rapids: Zondervan Publishing House, 1987.

Watson, Gary. "Skepticism about Weakness of Will." The *Philosophical Review* 86 (1977): 316–39.

Wesley, John. *The Works of John Wesley.* Vols. 6 and 9. Grand Rapids: Zondervan, 1872.

Willard, Dallas. *The Spirit of the Disciplines.* San Francisco: HarperCollins, 1988.

Wood, J. A., ed. *Christian Perfection as Taught by John Wesley.* Chicago: Christian Witness, 1885.

Index

Adam, 88, 91–92, 102
akrasia, akrates, 38–40, 62, 69–90,
 95–97, 100, 103–4, 146,
 151n. 28, 154n. 1, 156n. 34;
 Aristotelian approach to problem of, 72–74; biblical reflections on, 81–85; contemporary
 accounts of, 74–81; definition
 of, 38; distinguished from
 hypocrisy, 38; natural causes of,
 95–96; philosophical problem
 of, 69–70; Socratic approach to
 problem of, 69–73, 75; strategies for avoiding, 96–100; tendency toward. *See* sin, original
Alcott, Amos Bronson, 13
amoralism, 34–37, 66–69, 117, 119,
 123, 150n. 21, 151n. 24
apologetics, 10, 69, 126–27, 131,
 134, 144, 146–47
Aquinas, Thomas, 20–22, 88, 120
Arendt, Hannah, 105, 123
Aristotelian, 72–74, 77, 84, 86, 96,
 106, 110–12, 120, 122, 146
Aristotle, 36, 70, 72–75, 77, 81, 95,
 97–98, 110–11, 140, 151n. 28,
 152n. 1, 155n. 7, 158n. 25,
 160n. 14
Arminianism, 84–85
asceticism, 142

Assemblies of God, 103, 159n. 44
Audi, Robert, 63
Augustine, 88
autonomy, 26, 108–9
avowal, disavowal, 45, 60–66, 68,
 145, 154n. 40

bad faith, 22–23, 46–47, 64
Barrett, Boyd, 99
Baruch, Bernard, 145
Bayle, Pierre, 108
Benn, Piers, 40, 114, 121
Bentham, Jeremy, 107
biblical morality, 111, 143,
 160n. 16
Brothers Karamazov (Dostoevski),
 113
Buddha, 134
Buddhism, 129, 142
Butler, Joseph, 22, 33, 37

Calvin, John, 89, 124, 158n. 37
Calvinism, 84–85
Canfield, John, 52–54
Carlyle, Thomas, 145
Cartesian, 55–56
categorical imperative, 109, 119,
 160n. 12, 160n. 16
Catholic. *See* Roman Catholicism
causal necessity, 92–94

Cervantes, 44
Christ, Jesus, 10, 38–39, 43, 61, 81, 83, 100, 128, 133–35, 137, 139–41, 143–44, 146, 162n. 5
Christianity, 126–27, 129–32, 134, 137–39, 142, 147, 162n. 5, 163n. 11. *See also* Christian theism
Christian theism, 127, 134–35, 137, 141–42, 163n. 26. *See also* Christianity
church, 9–10, 14–15, 24, 88, 103, 108, 138, 140, 142–44, 146–47
civic-mindedness, 15, 122, 125
cognition, 27–28, 30, 40, 45, 58, 62–65, 67, 80, 86–87, 95, 145–46, 161n. 20
compartmentalism. *See* self-deception
compatibilism, 94
compulsion, 68, 73–75, 80, 90–93
conscience, 15, 89
conscientiousness, 121, 125
consequentialism, 111, 116–18, 160n. 12
continence, 72–73, 76–77
Cowton, Christopher, 30–34, 119, 150n. 3, 150n. 4, 150n. 5
crime, 17, 45, 53, 57, 117, 123
Crisp, Roger, 30–34, 119, 150n. 3, 150n. 4, 150n. 5

da Costa, Newton, 57
David, 18–19, 21, 31, 88, 121, 149n. 4
David Copperfield (Dickens), 16
Davidson, Donald, 76–77, 155n. 2
deception. *See* lying; self-deception
delusion, 33, 47, 121
Demos, Raphael, 33, 47–48, 152n. 10
deontological, 106, 108, 112, 117
Descartes, Rene, 55–56
determinism, 93–95
Dickens, Charles, 16
disavowal. *See* avowal, disavowal

discipline, 77, 97, 100, 142, 158n. 27; behavioral, 98; mental, 98; spiritual, 98, 142, 158n. 27
dispensationalism, 102, 159n. 39, 159n. 41
Dostoevski, Fyodor, 113
Dostoevskian, 117, 150n. 21
duty, 21, 35, 76, 106, 108, 110, 112, 124, 160n. 12
Dworkin, Ronald, 122

Edwards, Jonathan, 89, 91
egkrates. *See* continence
Eliot, George, 68
Epicureanism, 107
epistemology, 39, 45, 52, 55, 57, 62, 66, 127, 138, 152n. 11
ethics, 31, 36, 39, 43, 74, 100, 105–8, 111–12, 115, 117–18, 120, 124–25, 146, 160n. 14, 160n. 16. *See also* moral
eudaimonia, 110
evil, 10, 16–17, 21, 40–41, 70–71, 83, 88–89, 91, 123, 158n. 25

faith, 126, 129, 132–35, 137, 139–42, 144, 146–47, 162n. 5, 162n. 6
fallacy: of division, 93; genetic, 114; hypothesis contrary to fact, 138
Fingarette, Herbert, 48, 60–64
forgiveness, 15, 100, 136, 141
fraud, 17, 40, 131, 147
freedom, free will, 55–56, 69, 90–91, 93–95, 102, 129, 132, 146. *See also* volition
French, Steven, 57

Glaucon, 20, 116–17
glorification, 102
God, 43, 83, 85, 88–90, 92, 100–104, 106, 108, 111, 113, 124, 129, 135–37, 139, 142, 146, 158n. 37, 159n. 41, 162n. 5, 162n. 6

Goethe, 134
Golden Rule, 108, 160n. 12
grace, 61, 101–2, 135, 142–43, 147, 158n. 36
Gustavson, Don, 52–54

Hales, Steven, 59–60
Hare, R. M., 74–77, 81, 155n. 17
Hawthorne, Nathaniel, 15
hedonism, 71, 107, 155n. 3
Heep, Uriah, 16–21, 23, 118
Hegel, G. W. F., 21
Heine, Heinrich, 97
Hick, John, 128–32, 134–35
Hinduism, 129
Holy Spirit, 37, 85, 89, 91, 100, 102–3
honesty, 120, 123, 125, 141, 146, 151n. 30
House of the Seven Gables (Hawthorne), 15–16
Hume, David, 128, 130–32, 134–35
Huxley, Aldous, 44
hypocrisy: apologetic problem of, 126–44; of blame, 30–33; of complacency, 30–33; of inconsistency, 30–33; internal, 22–23, 33; as metavice and vice, 36–37; moral assessment of, 112–23; of pretense, 30–33, 120; roots of, 33–36; social benefits of, 40–42, 115; why Christians are prone to accusations of, 141–44
inconsistency, 19, 21, 25, 27–33, 35, 37, 39–40, 43, 48, 68, 116, 128, 133, 145; hypocrisy of (*see* hypocrisy); taxonomy of, 27–30
incontinence, 72–74, 76–80, 90, 151n. 28, 154n. 1. *See also akrasia*
integrity, 40, 61, 122–25, 145–46, 161n. 31
intention, 16, 20–21, 23, 29, 47–48, 55, 57–58, 60, 64–65, 69–71, 76, 78–80, 82, 97–99, 103, 117–18, 120, 124, 140–41

irony, ironic figures, 42–43, 151n. 31, 151n. 33
Islam, 129, 139

James, William, 98, 158n. 25
Jerome, 126
Johnston, Mark, 51, 58–60
Judaism, 84, 129–30, 139, 142, 160n. 12
justice, 20, 32, 48, 88, 116, 121, 125, 146, 160n. 12

Kant, Immanuel, 108–9, 119, 159n. 8, 160n. 12, 160n. 16
Kantian, 106, 108, 111–12, 117–18, 122, 124, 139, 146, 160n. 12, 160n. 14, 160n. 16
Keswickwian, 103
King-Farlow, John, 78–80
Kittay, Eva, 118, 151n. 31

La Rochefoucauld, Fracois, 105
Lewis, C. S, 123, 137–38
libertarianism: and freedom, 93–94; and political philosophy, 26, 29, 39–40
Lloyd-Jones, Martin, 84
Luther, Martin, 25, 84, 88–89
lying: to oneself, 22, 33, 46–48, 51, 54, 113, 152n. 10 (*see also* self-deception); to others, 20–21, 25, 28–29, 46–47, 120, 123, 160n. 12
Mandeville, Bernard, 41
McKinnon, Christine, 35, 42, 114, 118, 121, 161n. 24, 161n. 31
Mele, Alfred, 56–58, 63–64
mental sickness, 49
mental subsystem, 50, 57–60
mental system, 50–51
mental tropisms, 58–60
metaethics, 106, 111, 118
Mill, John Stuart, 107–8
Moliere, 14, 30
Moo, Douglas, 84
moral: community, 34–35, 40, 114, 119; depravity, 89, 91; free-

loading, 123; free-rider, 114, 121; ideals, 10, 31, 38, 43, 114–15, 133–34, 141–42; impostors, 41, 119, 143; improvement, 37, 101, 103–4, 136–39, 146 (*see also* sanctification); insight, poor, 39–40, 43; law, 21, 35, 37, 44, 85, 88, 117–19, 122–24, 136–37, 142, 145, 150n. 20, 151n. 24; nihilism (*see* amoralism); redemption, 37, 127, 135–40; regression, 137, 139–40; responsibility, 61, 90–91; seriousness, 34–36, 38, 41, 43–44, 67–68, 105, 113, 117, 119, 121, 143, 145–47; skepticism (*see* skepticism); theories, 106–11; weakness (*see akrasia*)
motivated bias. *See* self-deception

naturalism, 131
necessity. *See* causal necessity
Nietzsche, Friedrich, 36–37

obligation, 29, 35, 106, 108–9, 121, 123, 160n. 12
Ockham's razor, 79
original sin. *See* sin, original
Ovid, 68

Paluch, Stanley, 52, 152n. 2
Paul, 43, 82–84, 88, 90–91, 98, 100, 103, 140, 156n. 40, 156n. 41
Pears, David, 50–51, 60, 79–80
Penelhum, Terence, 53–54
Peter, 18–19, 38–39, 81–82, 95, 100, 143
Peterman, James, 55–56, 63–64
Pharisees, 30, 32, 39, 41–42, 105, 117–18, 121, 161n. 32
Plato, 20–21, 70–71, 110, 116, 155n. 5
psyche, 23, 33, 49, 152n. 13
psychoanalytic, 22, 49
psychopathology, 49
Pyncheon, Judge Jaffrey, 15–20, 23, 120–21

religion, 10, 14, 25, 42, 60, 108, 111, 124, 127–35, 142–44, 147, 159n. 8, 162n. 5, 163n. 11
religious exclusivism, 127–30, 134–35, 162n. 5
religious inclusivism, 162n. 5
religious pluralism, 127–28, 135, 162n. 5, 163n. 11
repentance, 15, 17–19, 21, 38, 72, 100, 136, 139–40, 143, 158–59n. 37
repression, 49–50, 59
Republic (Plato), 20, 116
revelation, divine, 106, 111
righteousness, 9, 20–21, 32, 35–36, 39, 89, 115, 119, 121, 127; imputed and infused, 101; nature and status of, 101–2
ring of Gyges, the myth of, 116
Roberts, Robert, 99, 161n. 25
Roman Catholicism, 101–2, 158n. 36
Rorty, Amelie, 50–51, 95–96, 98, 100, 153n. 19, 154n. 43
Rousseau, Jean Jacques, 108
Russell, Bertrand, 128, 133–35, 144
Ryle, Gilbert, 23, 73

salvation, 61, 128, 131, 142–43, 147, 162n. 5
sanctification, 24, 37, 87, 100–104, 136, 146, 158n. 37, 159n. 39, 159n. 41; definition of, 100–101; definitive and progressive, 102; entire, 103, 159n. 43; views of, 100–102
Sartre, Jean Paul, 22–23, 46–48, 61, 64
Saul, 17–19, 31, 39, 121
self-absorption and self-ignorance, 22, 37
self-command, 52–54, 75, 99
self-control, 38, 62, 77–81, 87, 96–100, 103, 146–47, 158n. 27
self-deception
    global and local, 35–36
    two phases of, 64–67

strategies to solve paradox of: epistemic strategies, 52–55; existential strategy, 60–62; moderate strategies, 55–60; partitioning strategies, 46–52

theories of: appeals to motivated bias, 55–58; appeals to subconscious processes, 58–60; compartmentalism, 48–52; lying to oneself, 46–48

self-indulgence, 72, 158n. 25

self-respect, 113

self-trickery, 98–99

Seneca, 87

Shakespeare, William, 13

Shaw, George Bernard, 25

Siegler, F. A., 54–55

sin, 10, 18, 24, 31, 37, 39, 83–85, 87–95, 99–103, 106, 115, 123–24, 136–39, 141–43, 146–47, 149n. 4; original, 85, 88–95, 102–3, 136; and sinful nature, 81–83, 90–95, 99, 143

sincerity, 40, 118–19, 123, 141

skepticism: global and local, 127; moral, 67, 114–15, 123; pyrrhonistic, 130–33; and objection from hypocrisy (see hypocrisy, apologetic problem of)

Sklar, Judith, 31, 150n. 12

Socrates, 42, 70–71, 107, 116, 134, 151n. 28, 155n. 3, 155n. 5

Socratic, 42, 69–73, 75–76, 80–85, 146, 151n. 28, 155n. 3, 155n. 5

soul, 49, 70, 72, 74, 85–86, 89, 101

"spelling out," 60–62, 64–66

Stocker, Michael, 79–80, 82

subconscious, 58–59, 114

subpersona, 78–79

sufficient reason, principle of, 94

Szabados, Bela, 33

Tartuffe, 14–20, 23, 30, 117, 120–21

teleology, 106–7, 111–12, 159n. 1

televangelists, 31, 126

temperance, 72, 111, 131

temptation, 26–27, 29, 38–39, 78, 80, 92, 95–100, 139, 143, 157n. 20

universalism, 117, 119, 125, 160n. 12, 160n. 16

utilitarianism, 41, 106–8, 110–12, 115–17, 124, 146, 159n. 4, 160n. 12, 160n. 14, 161n. 20

vice, 10, 13, 19–20, 22, 24, 27, 29–34, 36, 39–41, 43–44, 71–72, 77, 95, 98, 105, 110–13, 116–18, 123–25, 130, 138, 140, 144–47, 158n. 25, 160n. 14; first order, 36–37, 43–44, 145, 161n. 31; second order, 34, 36–37, 43–44, 145, 161n. 31

virtue, 15, 20–21, 31–32, 40–41, 43, 77, 87, 89, 95–98, 100–101, 103, 105–6, 110–12, 118, 120–23, 125, 144, 146, 150n. 4, 158n. 25, 158n. 27, 160n. 12, 160n. 14, 161n. 31

virtue theory, 80, 106, 110–12, 120–23

volition, 21, 45, 62–65, 145. See also freedom, free will

Voltaire, 108

Watson, Gary, 77–78, 80

weakness of will. See akrasia

Wesley, John, 89, 102, 159n. 43

Wesleyan view of sanctification, 102–3

Wilde, Oscar, 87

Zossima, 113

James S. Spiegel is an associate professor of philosphy at Taylor University in Upland, Indiana. He holds a Ph.D. degree in philosophy from Michigan State University.